100 Little Language Lessons

Skill-building activities featuring
600 essential vocabulary words

Written by Margaret Brinton

Illustrated by Len Shalansky

Teaching & Learning Company

1204 Buchanan St., P.O. Box 10
Carthage, IL 62321-0010

This book belongs to

Cover design by Sara King

Copyright © 2003, Teaching & Learning Company

ISBN No. 1-57310-410-8

Printing No. 98765432

Teaching & Learning Company
1204 Buchanan St., P.O. Box 10
Carthage, IL 62321-0010

Table of Contents

Dear Teacher or Parent,

In writing *100 Little Language Lessons*, I wanted to create a resource book that would not only educate your students but entertain them as well. I spent my time developing reading passages that I felt your students could readily relate to and enjoy. I devised a format for all of the lessons that would be predictable and easy to grasp. I have found, while using this manuscript with my own students, that the children are eager to take on each lesson. I hope that you will, likewise, observe that your own students will enjoy the lessons, find a challenge that supports their needs and reach satisfying levels of success in using *100 Little Language Lessons*.

I would suggest giving a spelling pre-test prior to each lesson, and giving a spelling post-test to each lesson would fully round out the session. To further expand each lesson, a post-lesson dictation exercise of the entire reading passage would be an excellent reinforcement. But don't stop there! Allow your students time to also make their own sentences. Have fun and enjoy each lesson in an interactive way!

Sincerely,

Margaret

Margaret Brinton

Pick a Pet

Find the meaning of each underlined word. Write the letter of the answer on the line.

Pick a turtle for a pet. It cannot run, but it can crawl (____).

Pick a rabbit for a pet. It can jump and bounce (____).

Pick a bird for a pet. It will sing a lovely song (____).

Pick a mouse for a pet. It has teeth to nibble (____).

Pick a puppy for a pet. It will be your friend and companion (____).

Pick a kitten for a pet. It feels soft and silky (____).

a. to go up and down
b. to move slowly
c. a buddy

d. smooth
e. to eat a little
f. pretty

....

Spell each word two times at the right.

1. crawl   _____   _____

2. bounce   _____   _____

3. lovely   _____   _____

4. nibble   _____   _____

5. companion   _____   _____

6. silky   _____   _____

....

Complete each idea with one new word.

1. To take a small bite   _____

2. To move like a snail   _____

3. A good pal   _____

4. Not rough or bumpy   _____

5. To move like a rubber ball _____

6. Beautiful   _____

Name _____

In Print

Find the meaning of each underlined word. Write the letter of the answer on the line.

Read, read, read. Read a book. Read a story. Just read! Read about rockets that blast to the sky (____). Read about whales that dive to the depths (____). Read about cotton that grows on plantations (____). Read about trees that cleanse our air (____). Read about clouds that contain the rain (____). Read about planes that transport people (____). Just read!

a. deep places
b. to carry a load
c. to take off fast

d. large farms
e. to hold inside
f. to make clean

....

Spell each word two times at the right.

1. blast   _____   _____

2. depths   _____   _____

3. plantations   _____   _____

4. cleanse   _____   _____

5. contain   _____   _____

6. transport   _____   _____

....

Complete each idea with one new word.

1. To remove dirt   _____

2. Large places for growing crops   _____

3. To leave the ground, like a rocket _____

4. To keep in   _____

5. To give a ride   _____

6. Deepness   _____

6

Name _____

A Boat Ride

Find the meaning of each underlined word. Write the letter of the answer on the line.

My uncle said, "Let's take a boat ride—not in a fast boat, not in a slow boat, but in a sailboat! Put on the life jacket, and <u>secure</u> the belt (____). Be careful when you step into the boat because it <u>wobbles</u> (____)! Find a place to sit, and <u>remain</u> in that spot (____). Now, we wait for the wind to lift the sails and put us in <u>motion</u> (____). There! Do you feel it? That wind is nice and <u>refreshing</u> (____)! We are off on our <u>journey</u> (____)!"

a. to stay
b. a trip
c. to feel fresh again

d. to shake
e. movement
f. to close tightly

Spell each word two times at the right.

1. secure   _____   _____

2. wobbles   _____   _____

3. remain   _____   _____

4. motion   _____   _____

5. refreshing   _____   _____

6. journey   _____   _____

Complete each idea with one new word.

1. Feeling good again   _____

2. To continue to be in the same place   _____

3. Pack your bags for this.   _____

4. Not loose   _____

5. An action   _____

6. To tip and bump   _____

A Soft Sofa

Find the meaning of each underlined word. Write the letter of the answer on the line.

A sofa is a wonderful place to sit and to rest. It has nice, soft <u>cushions</u> and maybe a pillow or two (____). You can lay your head back, and put your feet up. You can even close your eyes and <u>snooze</u> (____)! On a sofa, you can take a <u>moment</u> or two to rest (____). You can sit up and <u>chat</u> with a friend (____). You can lie down and nap. You can even <u>skim</u> the comics or read a book (____)!

A sofa is a <u>delight</u> (____)!

a. to take a look at
b. a short period of time
c. to talk together

d. cloth seats
e. a pleasure
f. to sleep

....

Spell each word two times at the right.

1. cushions   _____   _____

2. snooze   _____   _____

3. moment   _____   _____

4. chat   _____   _____

5. skim   _____   _____

6. delight   _____   _____

....

Complete each idea with one new word.

1. Take a rest   _____

2. Friendly conversation _____

3. Pleasing   _____

4. A kind of pillow   _____

5. To look over   _____

6. Not so long   _____

8

Study Hour

Find the meaning of each underlined word. Write the letter of the answer on the line.

Get ready to study. Here is what you will need.

1. a glass of water   Have a drink if you get <u>thirsty</u> (_____).

2. a pencil   Be sure the tip is <u>pointed</u> (_____).

3. an eraser   <u>Remove</u> any bad spots (_____).

4. a notebook   Do your work, and <u>organize</u> it (_____).

5. a note pad   Spell your words on the pad. Then <u>transfer</u> them to the notebook (_____).

6. a clock   Rest when you <u>notice</u> that one hour is done (_____).

a. put in good order	d. with a sharp tip
b. to see something	e. to take away
c. needing to drink	f. to change the place

Spell each word two times at the right.

1. thirsty   _____   _____

2. pointed   _____   _____

3. remove   _____   _____

4. organize   _____   _____

5. transfer   _____   _____

6. notice   _____   _____

Complete each idea with one new word.

1. To use the eyes   _____

2. Do not keep   _____

3. A feeling   _____

4. A pencil that is ready for writing   _____

5. Do not make a mess   _____

6. Make a change   _____

Name _____

Space Talk

Find the meaning of each underlined word. Write the letter of the answer on the line.

Do you want to go up in a rocket? You can fly to the moon and see how deep a crater is (____). You can pick up some moon soil from the ground (____). You can stand on the moon and look at the Earth. See what a beautiful globe the Earth is (____)! Now, take a moon rock in your hand. Take it home for your collection (____). Now, go back to the rocket. Strap into your seat (____). Fly back to Earth, and call a reporter (____)!

a. dirt
b. to buckle up
c. a news person

d. a big hole
e. a large ball
f. a set of things

....

Spell each word two times at the right.

1. crater   _____ _____

2. soil   _____ _____

3. globe   _____ _____

4. collection   _____ _____

5. strap   _____ _____

6. reporter   _____ _____

....

Complete each idea with one new word.

1. It's very round   _____

2. I give the news   _____

3. Hole caused by a meteorite _____

4. Lots of stuff   _____

5. To hold in place   _____

6. Different from sand   _____

Moon Rocks

Find the meaning of each underlined word. Write the letter of the answer on the line.

What are moon rocks like? Are they very hard and <u>rough</u> (____)? Are they thin and flat? Are they thick and <u>heavy</u> (____)? You can go to the library and get a book about moon rocks. Read the book to get more <u>information</u> (____). Find out all that you can. Then choose another book to <u>gain</u> more information (____). Keep reading! Keep <u>seeking</u> to know more (____). If you want to know more about moon rocks, study hard and you can become an <u>astronaut</u> and go to the moon (____)!

a. not soft
b. a space man (or woman)
c. to get

d. weighing a lot
e. facts to know
f. looking for

Spell each word two times at the right.

1. rough   _____   _____

2. heavy   _____   _____

3. information   _____   _____

4. gain   _____   _____

5. seeking   _____   _____

6. astronaut   _____   _____

Complete each idea with one new word.

1. Not to lose   _____

2. Space explorer   _____

3. What you learn   _____

4. Trying to find   _____

5. Having much weight   _____

6. Sandpaper feels like this _____

Name _____

Clean Your Plate

Find the meaning of each underlined word. Write the letter of the answer on the line.

Yesterday Mom took me to the doctor. The doctor said, "Do you always clean your plate?"

"Do you mean wash my plate?" I asked the doctor.

The doctor said, "No!

I mean, do you eat your vegetables (____)?" Then the doctor said, "Eat orange carrots, but

cut off the stem (____). Eat green lettuce, but always rinse it in water first (____). Eat a

red tomato, but let your mother slice it (____). Eat a green pepper, but not the entire thing

(____)."

Now I realize what "clean your plate" means (____)!

a. to wash
b. all of it
c. plants grown for food

d. the long, main part of a plant
e. to understand
f. to cut into thin, flat pieces

Spell each word two times at the right.

1. vegetables   _____   _____

2. stem   _____   _____

3. rinse   _____   _____

4. slice   _____   _____

5. entire   _____   _____

6. realize   _____   _____

Complete each idea with one new word.

1. Use a knife.   _____

2. To become aware   _____

3. Make it clean   _____

4. All, complete   _____

5. Plant part   _____

6. Not fruits   _____

Name _____

Important Date

Find the meaning of each underlined word. Write the letter of the answer on the line.

Monday, May 2:   Do my spelling words. <u>Memorize</u> them (____)!

For math class, fill in my <u>worksheets</u> (____).

Tuesday, May 3:   The sun was bright today. Write down the <u>temperature</u> (____).

Wednesday, May 4:   Read in my science book about how seeds <u>sprout</u> (____).

Thursday, May 5:   Get ready for Friday. I have a spelling <u>examination</u> (____).

Friday, May 6:   Get out my art paper, and <u>sketch</u> something (____).

a. class papers
b. test
c. to begin to grow

d. measure of heat or cold
e. to learn by heart
f. to make a picture

....

Spell each word two times at the right.

1. memorize   _____ _____

2. worksheets   _____ _____

3. temperature   _____ _____

4. sprout   _____ _____

5. examination   _____ _____

6. sketch   _____ _____

....

Complete each idea with one new word.

1. Summer heat or winter cold   _____

2. I do this just for fun   _____

3. I will pass it   _____

4. I will not forget   _____

5. The seeds open   _____

6. Practice pages   _____

Board Talk

Find the meaning of each underlined word. Write the letter of the answer on the line.

"Good morning, boys and girls. Please <u>prepare</u> your paper and pencil (____). We are going to make pictures from important shapes. First, I want you to draw a square. Put it anywhere on your paper that you would like. Now watch me <u>carefully</u> (____). See how I make my lines. The lines must be <u>straight</u> (____). See how I <u>connect</u> my lines (____). Now I have a <u>cube</u> (____)! It is almost like <u>magic</u> (____)!

a. a box shape
b. to get ready
c. paying close attention

d. to put together
e. not bent
f. a trick

Spell each word two times at the right.

1. prepare   _____   _____

2. carefully   _____   _____

3. straight   _____   _____

4. connect   _____   _____

5. cube   _____   _____

6. magic   _____   _____

Complete each idea with one new word.

1. The shape of ice   _____

2. Watchfully   _____

3. Is this for real?   _____

4. Get your things   _____

5. Dot to dot   _____

6. In a line   _____

Name _____

In the Dirt

Find the meaning of each underlined word. Write the letter of the answer on the line.

Take time to watch an ant at work. Do not stand up. Get down on your <u>knees</u>
(____). See how many ants there are? They live together in a <u>colony</u> (____). They
<u>reside</u> together (____), and they <u>assist</u> each other (____). If there is a big job to do,
the ants follow their <u>leader</u>(____). They are not lazy. They get the job done! We
can learn something from them. We can learn to help each other. Then we, too, will
have a better world. So, let's team up! Share the <u>purpose</u> (____)!

a. the boss
b. to live
c. a plan

d. a big group
e. to help
f. part of the leg

Spell each word two times at the right.

1. knees _____ _____

2. colony _____ _____

3. reside _____ _____

4. assist _____ _____

5. leader _____ _____

6. purpose _____ _____

Complete each idea with one new word.

1. To share the work _____

2. Bend them! _____

3. Where ants live _____

4. A teacher or parent _____

5. To live in a house _____

6. A goal _____

Name _____

Silver or Gold?

Find the meaning of each underlined word. Write the letter of the answer on the line.

Which is your favorite color, silver or gold? They are both beautiful. They both shine, and more than that, they <u>sparkle</u> (____)! If the sun shines on silver and gold, they are more beautiful yet. You can have a real <u>coin</u> of silver or gold to spend (____). You can have a silver or gold party <u>decoration</u> (____). You can have a balloon of silver or gold to <u>celebrate</u> a party (____). Do you know that silver and gold come from the land? They are <u>treasures</u> of our land (____). We must <u>value</u> them (____).

a. piece of money
b. to enjoy
c. valuable things

d. a pretty thing
e. to shine a lot
f. to hold close

Spell each word two times at the right.

1. sparkle   _____   _____

2. coin   _____   _____

3. decoration   _____   _____

4. celebrate   _____   _____

5. treasures   _____   _____

6. value   _____   _____

Complete each idea with one new word.

1. A penny   _____

2. To have fun   _____

3. Things we love   _____

4. To be bright   _____

5. A balloon   _____

6. Appreciate   _____

16

Stretch It Out

Find the meaning of each underlined word. Write the letter of the answer on the line.

Get up! Get ready for school! But before you go, take time to stretch your body.
Your body has many <u>muscles</u> (____), and you need to stretch them. Then you can sit
in school all day and not be tired. So, stretch your arms. Stretch your legs. Stretch
your neck and <u>shoulders</u> (____). Bend over. Lift up. <u>Rotate</u> in a circle (____).
<u>Raise</u> your arms up high. Push a little. Pull a little. Now open your mouth and
<u>breathe</u> (____). Breathe again. Stand tall, and <u>head</u> for school (____).

a. to move around
b. to get air
c. to go that way

d. joint connecting arm to body
e. stretchy body parts
f. to lift

....

Spell each word two times at the right.

1. muscles   _____   _____

2. shoulders   _____   _____

3. rotate   _____   _____

4. raise   _____   _____

5. breathe   _____   _____

6. head   _____   _____

....

Complete each idea with one new word.

1. On my way   _____

2. How we get air   _____

3. These help us move   _____

4. Arm joints   _____

5. To not put down   _____

6. Make a circle   _____

A Messy Nest

Find the meaning of each underlined word. Write the letter of the answer on the line.

Mom says that I have a messy nest. I think she means my bedroom! What can I do? I will look around. Now I see! I can put my dirty socks in the <u>laundry</u> (____). I can put my books on the <u>shelf</u> (____). I can hang my jacket on a <u>hook</u> (____). I can pick up my toys and put them into a <u>chest</u> (____). I can cover my bed with a <u>quilt</u> (____). I like my bedroom now. I am <u>proud</u> of it (____)!

a. a curved piece of metal or plastic
b. a bed cover
c. a place to wash

d. a ledge
e. a large box
f. feeling good

....

Spell each word two times at the right.

1. laundry   _____   _____

2. shelf   _____   _____

3. hook   _____   _____

4. chest   _____   _____

5. quilt   _____   _____

6. proud   _____   _____

....

Complete each idea with one new word.

1. It is nice and warm   _____

2. Not a bad feeling   _____

3. Where to clean something   _____

4. It has a lid   _____

5. Not a hanger   _____

6. A flat surface used to store things   _____

18

A Deep Sleep

Find the meaning of each underlined word. Write the letter of the answer on the line.

To be able to do well in school, you must sleep well at night. Here are some tips to help you sleep well:

1. Take a warm bath. It will <u>relax</u> you before sleeping (_____).

2. Drink a <u>mug</u> of warm milk before sleeping (_____).

3. Do not run, jump or <u>tumble</u> before sleeping (_____).

4. Do not <u>swallow</u> any kind of cola before sleeping (_____).

5. Read from a good <u>novel</u> before sleeping (_____).

6. Smile, and put your <u>thoughts</u> on something happy (_____)!

a. to settle down
b. to roll around
c. what you think

d. to gulp
e. a heavy cup with a handle
f. a story

....

Spell each word two times at the right.

1. relax   _____   _____

2. mug   _____   _____

3. tumble   _____   _____

4. swallow   _____   _____

5. novel   _____   _____

6. thoughts   _____   _____

....

Complete each idea with one new word.

1. Take it easy   _____

2. In your brain   _____

3. It is fun to do   _____

4. It holds liquid   _____

5. It has an end   _____

6. To consume liquid   _____

Wash Before You Wear

Find the meaning of each underlined word. Write the letter of the answer on the line.

It is important to be clean, and you can help. Do you know how to wash your socks? You can learn to wash your <u>dirty</u> socks (____). Before you go to bed, put a little water in the sink. Make a little <u>suds</u> with soap (____). Now wash your socks very well. Then put your socks in <u>fresh</u> water (____). Now <u>squeeze</u> all of the water out of your socks (____). Lay them on a dry <u>towel</u> (____). They will dry <u>overnight</u> (____). Put them on your feet in the morning!

a. a big bath cloth
b. bubbles
c. during the night

d. unsoiled
e. compress
f. not clean

Spell each word two times at the right.

1. dirty   _____   _____

2. suds   _____   _____

3. fresh   _____   _____

4. squeeze   _____   _____

5. towel   _____   _____

6. overnight   _____   _____

Complete each idea with one new word.

1. Nice and clean   _____

2. Stained   _____

3. Use it after your bath   _____

4. When you are sleeping   _____

5. Made from soap   _____

6. This is how to get the water out   _____

Name _____

Pass Them On

Find the meaning of each underlined word. Write the letter of the answer on the line.

Every day you grow. You grow bigger and taller day by day. Do your shoes still fit? Do not throw them in the garbage (____). Someone can use them! Clean them up. Wipe them off (____). Put new laces in them (____). Give them to a sister or brother or neighbor (____). Do not be selfish (____). Remember! Someone can put more miles on those shoes (____)!

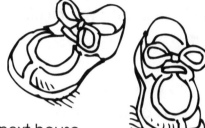

a. strings
b. trash
c. not able to share

d. to use a cloth
e. a person in the next house
f. 5280 feet

....

Spell each word two times at the right.

1. garbage   _____   _____

2. wipe   _____   _____

3. laces   _____   _____

4. neighbor   _____   _____

5. selfish   _____   _____

6. miles   _____   _____

....

Complete each idea with one new word.

1. A long way   _____

2. Old stuff   _____

3. A way to clean   _____

4. Just me, me, me   _____

5. Someone I know   _____

6. Cord used to tie shoes   _____

21

Name _____

Earth Love

Find the meaning of each underlined word. Write the letter of the answer on the line.

We have a beautiful Earth to live on! We have beautiful plants that blossom (____).
We have small hills and big mountains (____). We have rivers and lakes and puddles
from the rain (____). We have wet lands, but we also have dry deserts (____). We
have bugs in the gardens, and we have birds in the branches (____). We have animals all over the place! The Earth is full of variety (____)!

a. a pool of water
b. not all the same
c. parts of trees

d. to make flowers
e. huge hills
f. places of sand

....

Spell each word two times at the right.

1. blossom   _____   _____

2. mountains   _____   _____

3. puddles   _____   _____

4. deserts   _____   _____

5. branches   _____   _____

6. variety   _____   _____

....

Complete each idea with one new word.

1. Large hills   _____

2. An assortment of different things   _____

3. These grow from the main stem or trunk   _____

4. There is not much rain here   _____

5. A bird drinks from these   _____

6. To open up and grow   _____

Name _____

Do Pickles Grow?

Find the meaning of each underlined word. Write the letter of the answer on the line.

Do you like to eat pickles? Where do pickles come from? Do pickles grow in the garden (____)? Can you plant a pickle seed? Is there a pickle plant? Let me tell you about pickles! We buy pickles at the supermarket (____). We cannot get pickles from the garden. Then why is the pickle a food? It is because pickles are made from a garden plant called a cucumber (____). You can plant a cucumber seed; however, you cannot plant a pickle seed (____). A small cucumber makes a small pickle. A large cucumber makes an enormous pickle (____). What size pickle do you prefer (____)?

a. very big
b. but
c. a big food store

d. land used to grow flowers or vegetables
e. to like the best
f. a kind of food

Spell each word two times at the right.

1. garden   _____   _____

2. supermarket   _____   _____

3. cucumber   _____   _____

4. however   _____   _____

5. enormous   _____   _____

6. prefer   _____   _____

Complete each idea with one new word.

1. Where I plant seeds   _____

2. The plant that can become a pickle   _____

3. Where I can shop for food   _____

4. Not little   _____

5. To choose   _____

6. Not the same idea   _____

A Gray Day

Find the meaning of each underlined word. Write the letter of the answer on the line.

Sometimes I feel sad. That is what I call a Gray Day. Then I look for something to make me feel better. What do I do? I bake something! I bake cookies for dessert (____). I clean something! I scrub my bathroom sink (____). I make something! I use some clay and mold something (____). I share something! I look at what I have and divide it up (____). I love someone! I give someone a kiss on the cheek (____). I help someone! I aid anyone who needs me (____). There. Now it is not a Gray Day anymore!

a. a sweet food
b. part of the face
c. to clean hard

d. to make a shape
e. to separate into parts
f. to give help

Spell each word two times at the right.

1. dessert _____ _____

2. scrub _____ _____

3. mold _____ _____

4. divide _____ _____

5. cheek _____ _____

6. aid _____ _____

Complete each idea with one new word.

1. To make into sections _____

2. Assistance _____

3. To form or shape _____

4. Face part between nose and ear _____

5. Make it really clean _____

6. Maybe a cake _____

24

Little Brown Raisins

Find the meaning of each underlined word. Write the letter of the answer on the line.

Open a box of little brown raisins. Pop some in your mouth. <u>Chew</u> the sweet little things (____). Now think about this: Do raisins grow on trees like apples do? I can pick an apple from a tree. Can I pick a raisin? Try to <u>imagine</u> that (____)! It is funny! It is funny because raisins do not grow on trees. Raisins do not grow. Raisins come from <u>grapes</u> (____). Grapes grow! You can pick them from a <u>vine</u> (____). Then you can dry the grapes in the hot sun. When you dry the big grapes, they will <u>shrink</u> to little raisins (____). Now you have a very sweet <u>treat</u> (____)!

a. a kind of fruit
b. something good
c. to become smaller

d. bite and grind
e. to think about
f. a plant

Spell each word two times at the right.

1. chew _____ _____

2. imagine _____ _____

3. grapes _____ _____

4. vine _____ _____

5. shrink _____ _____

6. treat _____ _____

Complete each idea with one new word.

1. To form a mental picture _____

2. Use your teeth to grind _____

3. It is nice for me! _____

4. Something with juice inside _____

5. To shrivel in size _____

6. Melons and pumpkins grow on this _____

The Power of Rays

Find the meaning of each underlined word. Write the letter of the answer on the line.

Draw a picture of our sun. Start with a circle. Then make some lines. Those lines are called rays. Our sun has rays. We do not really see the rays, but we feel their power. The sun's rays are hot and bright (____). The rays reach all the way from the sun to the Earth (____). The rays give heat to our planet (____). The rays give warmth so that we do not feel cold (____). The rays help crops grow (____). The rays help grass and leaves to be healthy (____). We need the rays from our sun.

a. Earth
b. with a big shine
c. well and good

d. enough heat
e. plants grown on a farm
f. extend

....

Spell each word two times at the right.

1. bright _____ _____

2. reach _____ _____

3. planet _____ _____

4. warmth _____ _____

5. crops _____ _____

6. healthy _____ _____

....

Complete each idea with one new word.

1. Corn and apples _____

2. Brilliant _____

3. Not sick _____

4. A heavenly body, not a star _____

5. Not heat, not cold _____

6. From here to there _____

Name _____

What a Sense!

Find the meaning of each underlined word. Write the letter of the answer on the line.

I have a different sense in each different part of my body. In my eyes, I have the sense of sight (____). In my ears, I have the sense of hearing. In my mouth, I have the sense of taste. My tongue gives me the sense of taste (____). In my nose, I have the sense of smell. That is how I know one odor from another odor (____). My fingers give me the sense of touch (____). Sometimes a person will not have one sense or another sense. That can happen to a baby at birth (____). It can also happen from a bad accident (____).

a. when someone gets hurt
b. time to be born
c. a smell

d. part of the mouth
e. the ability to see
f. the ability to feel

....

Spell each word two times at the right.

1. sight

2. tongue

3. odor

4. touch

5. birth

6. accident

....

Complete each idea with one new word.

1. Something bad that happens

2. Vision

3. Scent

4. A new baby comes

5. How to know is something soft

6. It is close to my teeth

Name _____

How to Bank It!

Find the meaning of each underlined word. Write the letter of the answer on the line.

Do not spend all of your money! Try to save some of it. Here are some <u>suggestions</u> about how to save money (_____).

1. Put a little <u>plastic</u> dish by your bed. Put a little money in it each week (_____).

2. When the little plastic dish is full of money, <u>deposit</u> that money into a real bank (_____).

3. Start to fill your little <u>plastic</u> dish again (_____).

4. Put in a penny or two. Put in a big <u>quarter</u> (_____).

5. Keep filling your dish. Do not <u>permit</u> yourself to spend it (_____).

6. Now <u>pour</u> the money in a bag, and take it to the bank (_____).

a. ideas to share
b. to allow
c. not glass

d. 25 cents
e. make something flow
f. to put in a place

....

Spell each word two times at the right.

1. suggestions   _____   _____

2. plastic   _____   _____

3. deposit   _____   _____

4. quarter   _____   _____

5. permit   _____   _____

6. pour   _____   _____

....

Complete each idea with one new word.

1. One-fourth   _____

2. How to put the water from a bottle into a glass _____

3. Possibilities   _____

4. To put money into a bank account   _____

5. Most toys are made from this   _____

6. Mother said that I can   _____

  TLC10410 Copyright © Teaching & Learning Company, Carthage, IL 62321-0010

Name _____

The Old West

Find the meaning of each underlined word. Write the letter of the answer on the line.

Was it fun to be a cowboy? Was it fun to ride a horse across the <u>prairie</u> (____)?
Was it fun to sleep outside <u>beneath</u> the stars (____)? I think cowboy life was <u>excit-</u>
<u>ing</u> (____)! I think a cowboy had a good life. A cowboy could fish and <u>hunt</u> for
food (____). A cowboy could <u>roast</u> his food in the fire (____). A cowboy could also
swim in the lake and <u>bathe</u> in the river (____).

a. very fun
b. to take a bath
c. to search for something

d. grassland
e. to cook
f. under

....

Spell each word two times at the right.

1. prairie   _____   _____

2. beneath   _____   _____

3. exciting   _____   _____

4. hunt   _____   _____

5. roast   _____   _____

6. bathe   _____   _____

....

Complete each idea with one new word.

1. A large area of flat land with few or no trees _____

2. What to do if I am dirty   _____

3. Not on top   _____

4. To chase and kill an animal for food   _____

5. Wow! Wow! Wow!   _____

6. To prepare meat in a hot oven   _____

It Is O.K. to Nap

Find the meaning of each underlined word. Write the letter of the answer on the line.

Do you like to take a nap? I love to take a nap! A nap is not just for a baby. A nap is good for everybody. A nap will give you back energy (____). A good time to take a nap is after school. But do not doze too long (____). Just a short nap is best. Then get up and have a glass of water. Now you are ready to get your work done. You can do your homework assignment (____). You can make your bedroom tidy (____). You can match your socks for tomorrow (____). You can even have time to clip your fingernails (____).

a. a job to do
b. power
c. neat

d. to cut
e. to go together
f. to sleep

Spell each word two times at the right.

1. energy   _____   _____

2. doze   _____   _____

3. assignment   _____   _____

4. tidy   _____   _____

5. match   _____   _____

6. clip   _____   _____

Complete each idea with one new word.

1. Take a nap   _____

2. Homework   _____

3. Trim   _____

4. Make a pair   _____

5. Food and sleep give this to you   _____

6. Not messy   _____

Do Not Fear

Find the meaning of each underlined word. Write the letter of the answer on the line.

Oh, no! Do you have to take a test in school tomorrow? Do not fear! There is no need to be <u>frightened</u> about a test (_____). A test will not hurt you. A test will help you because you will <u>discover</u> what you do and do not know (_____). You can get ready to take a test. You can go to bed in the early <u>evening</u> (_____). You can eat a good <u>breakfast</u> the next day (_____). You can have a <u>chilled</u> glass of water (_____). Then your brain will be nice and <u>alert</u> (_____)! Do your best! Take the test!

a. very cold
b. night
c. awake

d. afraid
e. find out
f. the morning meal

Spell each word two times at the right.

1. frightened

2. discover

3. evening

4. breakfast

5. chilled

6. alert

Complete each idea with one new word.

1. Not sleepy

2. To learn

3. A time after afternoon

4. The first meal of the day

5. Sometimes like ice

6. If it scares me, I am _____

Name _____

Fine Foods

Find the meaning of each underlined word. Write the letter of the answer on the line.

Fish: Catch a fish from a <u>stream</u> and cook it (____).

Frankfurter: You need a very long bun for a <u>frankfurter</u> (____).

Float: Fill a glass with root beer and a <u>scoop</u> of ice cream to make a float (____).

Fruit: Put a fruit on ice cream to make a <u>sundae</u> (____).

Fast Food: A <u>tumbler</u> of milk is the best fast food (____).

French Fry: Cut a potato into <u>strips</u> to make French fries (____).

a. long pieces
b. a big spoonful
c. a tall glass

d. a hot dog
e. ice cream with a topping
f. a small river

....

Spell each word two times at the right.

1. stream   _____   _____

2. frankfurter   _____   _____

3. scoop   _____   _____

4. sundae   _____   _____

5. tumbler   _____   _____

6. strips   _____   _____

....

Complete each idea with one new word.

1. Not a cup   _____

2. A brook   _____

3. This can be eaten for dessert   _____

4. A long sausage, usually eaten on a bun _____

5. A big dip   _____

6. Long, thin pieces   _____

What's That Smell?

Find the meaning of each underlined word. Write the letter of the answer on the line.

Dad came into my bedroom and said, "What's that smell? Is there a dead mouse in the corner (____)? Is there old food that you forgot to dispose of (____)? Did you forget to throw away last week's lunch bags? What is causing that bad smell (____)?" So Dad and I began to search for the bad thing (____). Do you know what we found? We found my dirty socks! They were under the spread on my bed (____). Dad was very mad. I had to promise not to do that again (____).

a. to look
b. give your word
c. a warm cover

d. to put in the trash
e. making something happen
f. where two walls meet

....

Spell each word two times at the right.

1. corner   _____   _____

2. dispose   _____   _____

3. causing   _____   _____

4. search   _____   _____

5. spread   _____   _____

6. promise   _____   _____

....

Complete each idea with one new word.

1. Place where two sides come together   _____

2. A pledge   _____

3. To throw away   _____

4. I sleep under it   _____

5. Getting a result   _____

6. To try to find   _____

Trust Me

Find the meaning of each underlined word. Write the letter of the answer on the line.

My friend said to me, "Trust me!"

I said, "What does that mean?"

My friend told me, "I will always be your friend. You can <u>depend</u> on me (____). If you need someone to help you, I will be <u>available</u> (____). If you have a secret to tell, I will <u>protect</u> your secret (____). If you want to share an <u>activity</u>, just call me (____). <u>Whatever</u> you need, I will be there (____). Do not ever <u>worry</u> (____). Just trust me!"

a. to keep safe
b. not busy
c. count on

d. anything at all
e. be uneasy about
f. something fun to do

Spell each word two times at the right.

1. depend   _____   _____

2. available   _____   _____

3. protect   _____   _____

4. activity   _____   _____

5. whatever   _____   _____

6. worry   _____   _____

Complete each idea with one new word.

1. Able to use   _____

2. Maybe a game   _____

3. Any kind or type   _____

4. To guard   _____

5. To believe for sure _____

6. To feel nervous   _____

34

Storm Wind

Find the meaning of each underlined word. Write the letter of the answer on the line.

Most people hate storms. I don't hate storms, <u>though</u> (____). I like the <u>roar</u> of a storm (____). I like it when the wind <u>rattles</u> the doors and windows (____). I like it when the clouds <u>deliver</u> the rain (____). I like the sound of thunder and the flash of <u>lightning</u> (____). I like it when the rain turns to <u>hail</u> (____). But I do not want to be outside when it storms. I want to be safe at home!

a. a loud sound
b. to send
c. flash of light in the sky

d. shakes
e. however
f. small ice balls

....

Spell each word two times at the right.

1. though _____ _____

2. roar _____ _____

3. rattles _____ _____

4. deliver _____ _____

5. lightning _____ _____

6. hail _____ _____

....

Complete each idea with one new word.

1. The sound of a tiger _____

2. Frozen rain _____

3. Caused by electricity moving between clouds

   or between a cloud and the ground _____

4. But _____

5. What one snake does _____

6. To take something to someone _____

Name _____

Ups and Downs in Life

Find the meaning of each underlined word. Write the letter of the answer on the line.

1. a happy day/not <u>gloomy</u> (____)

2. a long lesson/not <u>brief</u> (____)

3. a deep lake/not <u>shallow</u> (____)

4. a sweet candy/not <u>tart</u> (____)

5. a hard carrot/not <u>tender</u> (____)

6. an easy test/not <u>tough</u> (____)

a. difficult
b. sour
c. short and quick

d. soft
e. sad
f. without depth

Spell each word two times at the right.

1. gloomy _____ _____

2. brief _____ _____

3. shallow _____ _____

4. tart _____ _____

5. tender _____ _____

6. tough _____ _____

Complete each idea with one new word.

1. Very hard _____

2. Easy to eat _____

3. Like a green apple _____

4. A rainy day feeling _____

5. Lasting only a short time _____

6. Like a puddle _____

36

Name _____

Animal Eyes

Find the meaning of each underlined word. Write the letter of the answer on the line.

Animals have different kinds of eyes. Think about these eyes of animals you know.

Cat: A cat has eyes that <u>gleam</u> with light in the night (____).

Eagle: An eagle has eyes that <u>detect</u> food a mile away (____).

Fish: A fish has eyes that see below the <u>surface</u> of the water (____).

Gorilla: A gorilla has black eyes that <u>blend</u> with his body (____).

Raccoon: A raccoon has eyes that <u>pierce</u> into the dark night (____).

Snake: A snake has eyes that do not have <u>lids</u> to close them (____).

a. to notice or to see
b. to match
c. a top or cover

d. to pass through
e. to shine
f. the top layer

....

Spell each word two times at the right.

1. gleam   _____   _____

2. detect   _____   _____

3. surface   _____   _____

4. blend   _____   _____

5. pierce   _____   _____

6. lids   _____   _____

....

Complete each idea with one new word.

1. To mix together well   _____

2. To poke a hole into   _____

3. Glow   _____

4. A box and a pan have these   _____

5. The flat part of a table   _____

6. To discover something   _____

Name _____

I Will Take Your Order Now

Find the meaning of each underlined word. Write the letter of the answer on the line.

We went to a <u>restaurant</u> to eat last night (_____). First, we sat down in a <u>booth</u> (_____). Then a man came and gave us a <u>menu</u> to look at (_____). Later, the <u>waiter</u> came and said, "I will take your order now (_____). I gave my order to the waiter. I said, "I'll have a <u>sausage</u> and rice dinner with a tall glass of milk (_____)." My dinner was <u>delicious</u> (_____)! I want to eat at that restaurant again!

a. a person who serves food
b. a place where people pay to eat meals
c. small, enclosed place

d. meat in a thin, tube-like casing
e. a list of foods
f. a very good taste

....

Spell each word two times at the right.

1. restaurant   _____   _____

2. booth   _____   _____

3. menu   _____   _____

4. waiter   _____   _____

5. sausage   _____   _____

6. delicious   _____   _____

....

Complete each idea with one new word.

1. A fast-food place   _____

2. Food server   _____

3. Like a hot dog   _____

4. A place to sit   _____

5. So good   _____

6. I can choose something to eat from this   _____

Lots of Action!

Find the meaning of each underlined word. Write the letter of the answer on the line.

Some words tell action. They are called <u>verbs</u> (____). To run, to walk, to jump are

some verbs that show action. Here are some others:

To <u>climb</u> a tall hill (____).

To <u>catch</u> a small bug (____).

To <u>twist</u> a long rope (____).

To <u>polish</u> a nice rock (____).

Now try to <u>create</u> your own list of action verbs (____).

a. to turn and wind
b. to grab or get
c. to rub something to make it shine

d. to make or design something
e. action words
f. to go up

....

Spell each word two times at the right.

1. verbs   _____   _____

2. climb   _____   _____

3. catch   _____   _____

4. twist   _____   _____

5. polish   _____   _____

6. create   _____   _____

....

Complete each idea with one new word.

1. These words show something to do   _____

2. Use your brain   _____

3. Use your legs and hands   _____

4. To twirl   _____

5. To make something shiny   _____

6. To get something you are chasing   _____

Bug World

Find the meaning of each underlined word. Write the letter of the answer on the line.

There are millions and billions of bugs in our world. We only see a few of them. The Earth has more bugs than people! So, where are the millions and billions of bugs? Green bugs hide in the turf (____). Yellow bugs hide in the leaves of autumn (____). Brown bugs hide on sticks on the ground and on the twig of a tree (____). Red bugs hide near the clay (____). But black bugs are sometimes easy to spot (____). Black bugs do not have many places to camouflage (____).

a. to disguise the skin color
b. to see
c. surface layer of grass and earth on a lawn

d. small, thin branches
e. mud for bricks
f. fall season

....

Spell each word two times at the right.

1. turf   _____   _____

2. autumn   _____   _____

3. twig   _____   _____

4. clay   _____   _____

5. spot   _____   _____

6. camouflage   _____   _____

....

Complete each idea with one new word.

1. An ant can sit on this   _____

2. Wet and sticky earth   _____

3. To not be seen   _____

4. A place to lie down   _____

5. To use my eyes   _____

6. After the summer   _____

Steel Tracks

Find the meaning of each underlined word. Write the letter of the answer on the line.

I love to ride the train! I love to hear the sound of the train on the tracks. It is a loud sound because the tracks are <u>constructed</u> from steel (____). Think about the men who <u>laid</u> those tracks (____). They were strong men. They had to <u>labor</u> very, very hard (____). That kind of work makes a man <u>sweat</u> (____). When my train goes on the tracks, I think about the men who did that work. Those men had <u>strength</u> (____). I <u>respect</u> their work (____).

a. put in place
b. built
c. perspire

d. to think well of
e. power
f. to work

· ·

Spell each word two times at the right.

1. constructed _____   _____

2. laid _____   _____

3. labor _____   _____

4. sweat _____   _____

5. strength _____   _____

6. respect _____   _____

· ·

Complete each idea with one new word.

1. Put something down _____

2. Put something together _____

3. Admire _____

4. To work hard _____

5. Being hot or nervous causes this _____

6. Force _____

After the Snack

Find the meaning of each underlined word. Write the letter of the answer on the line.

I am very <u>hungry</u> after school (____). I need a snack! I think I'll eat some toast with <u>marmalade</u> (____). That <u>flavor</u> is very, very good (____). Now, I have to do my work. For math class, I have to <u>calculate</u> 20 problems (____). For science class, I have to set up my <u>experiment</u> (____). For English class, I have to write a <u>paragraph</u> (____). When all of that is done, I will need another snack!

a. a scientific test
b. taste
c. a short passage in writing

d. needing to eat
e. to figure out by using arithmetic
f. orange jam

....

Spell each word two times at the right.

1. hungry   _____   _____

2. marmalade   _____   _____

3. flavor   _____   _____

4. calculate   _____   _____

5. experiment   _____   _____

6. paragraph   _____   _____

....

Complete each idea with one new word.

1. To use math   _____

2. When I want food   _____

3. A way to test a theory or see an effect   _____

4. A kind of jam   _____

5. One or more sentences about a single subject or idea _____

6. Maybe sweet, maybe sour   _____

U.F.O. in the Night

Find the meaning of each underlined word. Write the letter of the answer on the line.

I saw a light in the sky last night. My sister told me it was a U.F.O. I said to my sister, "What do the letters *U.F.O.* <u>represent</u> (____)?" She told me that *U.F.O.* represented <u>Unidentified</u> Flying Object (____). "Wow!" I said, "Do you think it is <u>creatures</u> from Mars (____)? Do you think they fly in an object like that? Do you <u>suppose</u> they are coming to visit us (____)?" Then my sister told me that she was just <u>teasing</u> me (____). She said, "It is <u>probably</u> just an airplane (____)."

a. to imagine something is possible
b. almost sure
c. not able to identify
d. stand for
e. living things
f. making a joke

Spell each word two times at the right.

1. represent   _____   _____

2. unidentified   _____   _____

3. creatures   _____   _____

4. suppose   _____   _____

5. teasing   _____   _____

6. probably   _____   _____

Complete each idea with one new word.

1. People or animals   _____

2. Not known   _____

3. Likely   _____

4. This makes me laugh or cry   _____

5. A picture can do this   _____

6. To believe or guess   _____

A Little Bird Sings

Find the meaning of each underlined word. Write the letter of the answer on the line.

I have a <u>canary</u> that lives in a cage (____). I love my little canary! She is just <u>delightful</u> (____). She sings such sweet music. Every day she sings a different <u>melody</u> (____). Some friends say that she just <u>chirps</u> (____). But I say, "No. That is her melody." She sings a melody better than I do. Sometimes I <u>practice</u> singing with her (____). Then we have a <u>duet</u> (____)!

a. a tune
b. a yellow bird
c. to make bird sounds

d. pleasing
e. two voices together
f. to try to learn

Spell each word two times at the right.

1. canary   _____   _____

2. delightful   _____   _____

3. melody   _____   _____

4. chirp   _____   _____

5. practice   _____   _____

6. duet   _____   _____

Complete each idea with one new word.

1. A song for two   _____

2. To improve a skill by doing over and over   _____

3. A musical phrase   _____

4. Noise a bird makes   _____

5. Very, very nice   _____

6. A small bird known for its singing   _____

Nice Nouns

Find the meaning of each underlined word. Write the letter of the answer on the line.

Do you know what a noun is? A noun is a word that is a person, place or thing. A noun is fun to find. Look at each noun below, and find the meaning of it.

1. a <u>mirror</u> to see into (____)

2. a <u>skillet</u> to fry in (____)

3. an <u>automobile</u> to drive (____)

4. a <u>mechanic</u> to talk to (____)

5. a <u>cricket</u> to catch (____)

6. an <u>avenue</u> to walk on (____)

a. a kind of bug
b. a street
c. a car

d. a person who fixes cars
e. a looking glass
f. a cooking pan

Spell each word two times at the right.

1. mirror   _____   _____

2. skillet   _____   _____

3. automobile   _____   _____

4. mechanic   _____   _____

5. cricket   _____   _____

6. avenue   _____   _____

Complete each idea with one new word.

1. It has six legs   _____

2. It has wheels   _____

3. It can crack   _____

4. Good for cooking eggs _____

5. He has tools   _____

6. A wide road   _____

Air Quick

Find the meaning of each underlined word. Write the letter of the answer on the line.

A very quick way to go to another place is by airplane. Did you ever <u>travel</u> in the air (____)? Did you like being <u>higher</u> than the clouds (____)? Did you like traveling at that fast <u>rate</u> (____)? Did you look down below and see green <u>pastures</u> (____)? To travel by airplane gets you there fast, <u>wherever</u> you want to go (____). I hope you have some money; it's <u>expensive</u> (____)!

a. up above
b. speed
c. any place

d. to take a trip
e. grass lands
f. high cost

....

Spell each word two times at the right.

1. travel

2. higher

3. rate

4. pastures

5. wherever

6. expensive

....

Complete each idea with one new word.

1. To move from one place to another

2. Cows eat here

3. How fast or how slow

4. Not cheap

5. Way, way up

6. Here or there

A Glass of Oxygen

Find the meaning of each underlined word. Write the letter of the answer on the line.

Do you know the best thing to drink if you are sick? A glass of water! If you are hot? A glass of water! If you are feeling tired? A glass of water! Water is full of oxygen! That is why I call it "a glass of oxygen!" So, if you drink water, the oxygen will <u>rush</u> into your body (____). Your blood <u>vessels</u> will carry the oxygen all around your body (____). Your brain will <u>receive</u> oxygen from the glass of water (____). The oxygen will help your brain to stay <u>vital</u> (____). So, have a glass of water! In fact, drink a <u>quart</u> of it (____)!. Your body will <u>appreciate</u> that (____)!

a. to feel thankful
b. to hurry
c. tubes

d. full of life, energy
e. four cups
f. to get something

Spell each word two times at the right.

1. rush   _____   _____

2. vessels   _____   _____

3. receive   _____   _____

4. vital   _____   _____

5. quart   _____   _____

6. appreciate   _____   _____

Complete each idea with one new word.

1. A unit of liquid measure   _____

2. To enjoy or value someone or something   _____

3. The opposite of *give*   _____

4. Very alive   _____

5. Blood moves in these   _____

6. To not go slowly   _____

Name _____

State Lines

Find the meaning of each underlined word. Write the letter of the answer on the line.

Do you know the 50 states in the U.S.? Can you name all of them? To name the 50 states is a <u>challenge</u> (____). Do you know something about Nevada? Part of Nevada is <u>arid</u> like a desert (____). Do you know New Mexico? It has a deep, deep <u>cavern</u> (____). Do you know that Iowa has very bad <u>tornadoes</u> (____)? Do you know that Maine has trees that give us <u>syrup</u> (____)? The U.S. has 50 great states! Try to learn something <u>factual</u> about each great state (____).

a. a large cave
b. true
c. whirling columns of air

d. dry
e. a hard job
f. sweet, thick liquid

··

Spell each word two times at the right.

1. challenge   _____   _____

2. arid   _____   _____

3. cavern   _____   _____

4. tornadoes   _____   _____

5. syrup   _____   _____

6. factual   _____   _____

··

Complete each idea with one new word.

1. Something that requires extra effort   _____

2. Not much water   _____

3. Not false   _____

4. Bats can live here.   _____

5. This has a good taste   _____

6. These look like dark, funnel-shaped clouds   _____

Name _____

Remember Me?

Find the meaning of each underlined word. Write the letter of the answer on the line.

Dear Sam,

I am on vacation with my family. We are in San Diego. We came here on Flight 217.
We had a nice <u>flight</u> (____). It was very <u>smooth</u> (____). We are at a good hotel near
the beach. I can smell salt in the ocean <u>breeze</u> (____). I saw three <u>dolphins</u> in the
ocean yesterday (____)! They were playing in the <u>surf</u> (____). Tomorrow we will get
on a bus at the San Diego Zoo and take a <u>tour</u> (____).

Your friend,

Ted

a. with no bumps
b. gentle wind
c. a trip to view something

d. ocean waves
e. a water mammal
f. airplane trip

Spell each word two times at the right.

1. flight   _____   _____

2. smooth   _____   _____

3. breeze   _____   _____

4. dolphins   _____   _____

5. surf   _____   _____

6. tour   _____   _____

Complete each idea with one new word.

1. Even and flat   _____

2. Waves as they break on the shore   _____

3. I can feel this on my face   _____

4. A sightseeing trip   _____

5. The ability to fly   _____

6. These sea animals are very intelligent _____

A Big Pot

Find the meaning of each underlined word. Write the letter of the answer on the line.

Mom has a big cooking pot! She can fix anything in that pot. Each day when I come home from school, I look in the pot. Then I see what is cooking. Sometimes I see a chicken in the pot. Then I know that we will have a <u>stew</u> (____). Sometimes I see pasta in the pot. Then I know that we will have <u>spaghetti</u> (____). Sometimes I see fruit in the pot. Then I know that Mom is making <u>preserves</u> (____). I want to cook in a big pot when I grow up. That will be an <u>adventure</u> (____). I will <u>simmer</u> good food in my pot (____). Then I can <u>please</u> my family just like Mom (____)!

a. jam
b. long, thin noodles
c. an exciting experience

d. to make someone happy
e. a dish of meat or fish and vegetables
f. to boil gently

....

Spell each word two times at the right.

1. stew   _____   _____

2. spaghetti   _____   _____

3. preserves   _____   _____

4. adventure   _____   _____

5. simmer   _____   _____

6. please   _____   _____

....

Complete each idea with one new word.

1. I put this on toast   _____

2. A great, fun time   _____

3. Made by cooking meat or fish with vegetables in liquid _____

4. To give a good feeling   _____

5. Noodles you can twist around your fork   _____

6. To cook by boiling gently   _____

Play the Big K

Find the meaning of each underlined word. Write the letter of the answer on the line.

K is for <u>kangaroo</u>. It can jump far (_____).

K is for <u>Kansas</u>. Some people live there (_____).

K is for <u>keyboard</u>. You can play on this (_____).

K is for <u>kelp</u>. It grows in water (_____).

K is for <u>kidney</u>. The doctor checks this (_____).

K is for <u>Kipling</u>. I love his stories (_____).

a. a set of keys on a computer, piano, etc.   d. a weed from the sea
b. a part of your body   e. a state in the U.S.
c. a great writer   f. an animal of Australia

....

Spell each word two times at the right.

1. kangaroo

2. Kansas

3. keyboard

4. kelp

5. kidney

6. Kipling

....

Complete each idea with one new word.

1. He wrote *The Jungle Book*

2. The female carries her baby in pocket!

3. Topeka is its capital

4. A fish can hide here

5. An organ inside the body

6. Some are *qwerty*

Do You Remember Marbles?

Find the meaning of each underlined word. Write the letter of the answer on the line.

Kids used to play with marbles a lot. Do you ever play with marbles? You can buy them at the toy store. You get a lot of them in one <u>pouch</u> (____). It is easy to carry a pouch of marbles. A pouch of marbles does not have much <u>weight</u> (____). So you can take your marbles <u>anywhere</u> (____). Take them to the park, and <u>exchange</u> some with your friend (____). Take them to the beach, and make a <u>pit</u> to roll them into (____). Count them. Line them up. <u>Separate</u> them by color (____). You will see how much fun a pouch of marbles can be.

a. a hole in the ground
b. a bag
c. to trade

d. to any place
e. divide
f. a measure of heaviness

⋯⋯⋯⋯⋯⋯⋯⋯⋯⋯⋯⋯⋯⋯⋯⋯⋯⋯⋯⋯⋯⋯⋯⋯⋯⋯⋯⋯⋯

Spell each word two times at the right.

1. pouch _____ _____

2. weight _____ _____

3. anywhere _____ _____

4. exchange _____ _____

5. pit _____ _____

6. separate _____ _____

⋯⋯⋯⋯⋯⋯⋯⋯⋯⋯⋯⋯⋯⋯⋯⋯⋯⋯⋯⋯⋯⋯⋯⋯⋯⋯⋯⋯⋯

Complete each idea with one new word.

1. Not put together _____

2. It can hold something _____

3. It is deep. _____

4. Swap _____

5. Here or there _____

6. Ten pounds _____

TLC10410 Copyright © Teaching & Learning Company, Carthage, IL 62321-0010

He Has Big Feet

Find the meaning of each underlined word. Write the letter of the answer on the line.

Did you ever go to a place called <u>Oregon</u> (_____)? People talk about a <u>monster</u> that lives there (_____). He has very big feet! People try to find his footprints in the snow. Then they <u>measure</u> his footprints (_____). His footprints are very, very big! That is why they call this monster Big Foot! But nobody can <u>capture</u> him (_____). He always has a way to <u>escape</u> (_____). So, people talk a lot about Big Foot. But nobody has any <u>proof</u> (_____).

a. a scary creature
b. to find out the size
c. a state in the U.S.

d. facts or evidence
e. to get away
f. to catch

. . . .

Spell each word two times at the right.

1. Oregon _____   _____

2. monster _____   _____

3. measure _____   _____

4. capture _____   _____

5. escape _____   _____

6. proof _____   _____

. . . .

Complete each idea with one new word.

1. To break free _____

2. To take by force _____

3. Salem is its capital _____

4. Something true _____

5. Not a person _____

6. To find the true size _____

Sandy Beach

Find the meaning of each underlined word. Write the letter of the answer on the line.

On a sunny day, the place I love to go to is the beach! I love any kind of beach. The beach by the lake, the beach by the river, the beach by the ocean, too (____). I love to feel the sand under my feet. I love to fill my hands with sand. It is fun to sprinkle the sand from my hands (____). I love to dig in the sand and find a secret thing there (____). Sometimes I find a penny in the sand. Sometimes I find a paper there with a message on it (____). Other times I watch a little crab try and burrow under the sand (____). Did you know a crab can exist under the sand (____)? Now, do you see why I just love the beach?

a. the sea
b. information sent to someone
c. to live

d. to dig
e. something hidden
f. to shake out a little

....

Spell each word two times at the right.

1. ocean   _____   _____

2. sprinkle   _____   _____

3. secret   _____   _____

4. message   _____   _____

5. burrow   _____   _____

6. exist   _____   _____

....

Complete each idea with one new word.

1. Private information   _____

2. A note   _____

3. Not to die   _____

4. It has salt water   _____

5. To make a tunnel or hole in the ground   _____

6. To scatter bit by bit   _____

Way, Way Down

Find the meaning of each underlined word. Write the letter of the answer on the line.

My friend's dad works in a silver mine. Every day he goes way, way down under a very big hill. He told me that his work is very dangerous (_____). He said that is why he can earn a lot of money (_____). He goes into the dark silver mine with several good lights (_____). Then he can find his way. There is no light from the sun down under the earth (_____). So it is cool and a little bit damp down there (_____). When his work is done, he is ready to find the passage and get back home (_____).

a. more than two
b. to get paid for work
c. slightly wet

d. the ground or land
e. hallway or corridor
f. not safe

· ·

Spell each word two times at the right.

1. dangerous

2. earn

3. several

4. Earth

5. damp

6. passage

· ·

Complete each idea with one new word.

1. A few

2. The planet where we live

3. Likely to cause injury or harm

4. Not dry

5. To get money for doing a job

6. Anything that allows you to pass from one place to another _____

Never Tip a Canoe

Find the meaning of each underlined word. Write the letter of the answer on the line.

Town News

Yesterday morning, two boys went to the lake. They got into a <u>canoe</u> that was near the water (_____). They were not thinking, and they made a very big <u>mistake</u> (_____). They <u>thought</u> they could take a ride in the canoe (_____). They thought they knew how to paddle. But it was a mistake. Someone on the <u>beach</u> saw the canoe tip over (_____). Someone said, "They will <u>drown</u> (_____)!" Lucky for the two boys, there was a man swimming in the lake. He was able to <u>rescue</u> them (_____).

a. to save a life
b. where the sand is
c. to die in the water

d. a narrow kind of boat
e. error
f. had an idea or opinion

....

Spell each word two times at the right.

1. canoe   _____   _____

2. mistake   _____   _____

3. thought   _____   _____

4. beach   _____   _____

5. drown   _____   _____

6. rescue   _____   _____

....

Complete each idea with one new word.

1. To die from lack of air when underwater   _____

2. It moves on the water with paddles.   _____

3. To help someone who is in danger   _____

4. Where to play   _____

5. Not the right thing to do   _____

6. Past tense of *think*   _____

Look at the Noun

Find the meaning of each underlined word. Write the letter of the answer on the line.

Do you know what a noun is? A noun is a person word like *mother* or *teacher* or *chef* (____). A noun is a place word like *house* or *lake* or _lawn_ (____). A noun is a thing word like *toy* or *book* or _sweater_ (____). A noun is an idea word like *joy* or *pain* or _happiness_ (____). It is fun to use nouns to write a good <u>sentence</u> (____). How many nouns can you <u>identify</u> in this sentence (____): The boy and his brother took apples and bread to school.

a. a knitted piece of clothing
b. a place with grass
c. words expressing a complete thought

d. recognize
e. a person who cooks
f. feeling pleased

Spell each word two times at the right.

1. chef   _____ _____

2. lawn   _____ _____

3. sweater   _____ _____

4. happiness   _____ _____

5. sentence   _____ _____

6. identify   _____ _____

Complete each idea with one new word.

1. Wear this if I am cold   _____

2. Chief cook in a restaurant   _____

3. To tell what something is   _____

4. A nice place to sit or play   _____

5. This must have noun and verb to be complete _____

6. A very good feeling   _____

A Tip or Two to Remember

Find the meaning of each underlined word. Write the letter of the answer on the line.

If it is a hot, summer day you need a tip or two to remember. The most important tip for a hot, summer day is to drink <u>plenty</u> of water (____). You can drink other <u>fluids</u>, too (____). Just drink, drink, drink. You need to drink because of the summer <u>heat</u> (____). There is another thing to remember about the summer. The sun is very <u>intense</u> (____). So, if you go outside, put on a hat. The hat will <u>shield</u> you from the sun's heat (____). A hat and plenty of fluids to drink will keep you safe. You will not <u>collapse</u> on a hot, summer day (____).

a. to fall down suddenly
b. to keep you safe
c. a lot

d. very strong
e. liquids
f. great warmth

Spell each word two times at the right.

1. plenty _____ _____

2. fluids _____ _____

3. heat _____ _____

4. intense _____ _____

5. shield _____ _____

6. collapse _____ _____

Complete each idea with one new word.

1. Not cold _____

2. Water and milk _____

3. A sudden failure _____

4. Powerful _____

5. More than enough _____

6. To protect _____

A Way to Fly

Find the meaning of each underlined word. Write the letter of the answer on the line.

Most birds can fly. They <u>flap</u> their wings to fly (____). Some birds do not have to flap all the time. They can just <u>glide</u> in the air (____). One bird that does not flap is the <u>hawk</u> (____). Up in the air the hawk can glide. It can glide high in the air and <u>scan</u> the world (____). Maybe there will be a mouse down below. Then the hawk will glide down and <u>grab</u> that mouse. The hawk has a <u>great</u> way to fly (____)!

a. to move smoothly and easily
b. very good
c. to move up and down

d. to take hold of
e. to look at quickly
f. a kind of hunting bird

Spell each word two times at the right.

1. flap

2. glide

3. hawk

4. scan

5. grab

6. great

Complete each idea with one new word.

1. Wonderful

2. Grasp

3. To read without looking for detail

4. To put the wings up and down

5. To ride on currents of air

6. A bird of prey

In the Night

Find the meaning of each underlined word. Write the letter of the answer on the line.

There are many animals that move in the night. Life at night is not <u>equal</u> to life in the day (____). Night life is dark and <u>quiet</u> (____). So animals that move in the night have to move in the dark. They have eyes that can <u>focus</u> in the dark (____). They have feet that can move and not make <u>noise</u> (____). They sleep in the daytime, so they are <u>ready</u> to move at night (____). Then they go home to sleep at <u>dawn</u> (____).

a. to adjust the eyes to see clearly
b. not loud
c. sound

d. the same
e. willing and able to do
f. when day begins

Spell each word two times at the right.

1. equal   _____   _____

2. quiet   _____   _____

3. focus   _____   _____

4. noise   _____   _____

5. ready   _____   _____

6. dawn   _____   _____

Complete each idea with one new word.

1. Something that you hear   _____

2. When the sun comes up   _____

3. To see well   _____

4. Prepared   _____

5. There is no noise   _____

6. Exactly alike   _____

60

Mind Me!

Find the meaning of each underlined word. Write the letter of the answer on the line.

My dad wants me to be my best. That is why he always says, "Mind me!" So, I try
to mind my dad. He is my dad, so I try to <u>obey</u> him (____). Dad tells me to go to
bed on time. I want to get <u>enough</u> sleep (____). So, I mind him! Dad tells me to do
my <u>homework</u> (____). I want to get good <u>grades</u> (____). So, I mind him! Dad tells
me to <u>finish</u> my milk (____). I want to have good <u>bones</u> (____). So I mind him!
I like to mind my dad!

a. to complete
b. to follow instructions
c. the work for school

d. parts of a skeleton
e. school marks
f. what I need

Spell each word two times at the right.

1. obey

2. enough

3. homework

4. grades

5. finish

6. bones

Complete each idea with one new word.

1. I do this after school

2. Not more, not less

3. Reach the end

4. To do what someone tells you

5. An adult human has 206 of these

6. A, B, C, D, F

Step It Up!

Find the meaning of each underlined word. Write the letter of the answer on the line.

Our teacher likes to have a nice room. We have to help her keep it nice. We clean and put away our things. If we are slow, our teacher says, "Step it up!" She does not want us to <u>waste</u> time (____). So, we move fast to get the job <u>done</u> (____). We pick our books up from the <u>floor</u> (____). We put our papers in a <u>stack</u> (____). We put our coats on the <u>rack</u> (____). Then the room looks clean and <u>neat</u> (____). Our teacher is ready to teach.

a. a place to walk upon
b. finished
c. tidy

d. not to use well
e. a place to hang something
f. a neat pile

Spell each word two times at the right.

1. waste _____ _____

2. done _____ _____

3. floor _____ _____

4. stack _____ _____

5. rack _____ _____

6. neat _____ _____

Complete each idea with one new word.

1. Not messy _____

2. Hang a hat or clothes here _____

3. No more to do _____

4. Flat surface for walking or standing _____

5. To place one on top of another _____

6. To use or spend foolishly _____

TLC10410 Copyright © Teaching & Learning Company, Carthage, IL 62321-0010

Front Page

Find the meaning of each underlined word. Write the letter of the answer on the line.

Read the <u>front</u> page (____). The front page has this to say:

There Will Be Sun <u>Tomorrow</u> (____)!

Spring Is Just <u>Thirteen</u> Days Away (____)!

Put Away Your Winter <u>Jacket</u> (____)!

Keep Your Boots for the <u>Mud</u> (____)!

Get Out Your Ball and <u>Mitt</u> (____)!

a. the day after today
b. short coat
c. 10 plus 3

d. not the back
e. baseball glove
f. wet dirt

Spell each word two times at the right.

1. front

2. tomorrow

3. thirteen

4. jacket

5. mud

6. mitt

Complete each idea with one new word.

1. Today plus one more day

2. Not sand

3. This protects the hand when playing ball

4. It keeps me warm

5. 7 plus 6

6. The part that comes first

A Good Note

Find the meaning of each underlined word. Write the letter of the answer on the line.

My teacher gave me a note. It was a good note. This is what my good note said:

Bob, your work at school is good. You are reading well. Your reading test <u>score</u> is 92 (____). Your math score is also <u>high</u> (____). It is 89. But in spelling you need to <u>improve</u> (____). Your spelling score is only 56. Try to copy your spelling words. Copy them five times <u>instead</u> of three times (____). That will help you <u>remember</u> them (____). Keep up your good work. I also like the way that you <u>behave</u> (____) in class.

From,

Miss King

a. to act
b. how many points
c. to get better

d. in place of
e. not forget
f. not low

Spell each word two times at the right.

1. score   _____ _____

2. high   _____ _____

3. improve   _____ _____

4. instead   _____ _____

5. remember   _____ _____

6. behave   _____ _____

Complete each idea with one new word.

1. A number in a game, contest or test   _____

2. In place of another   _____

3. Above the normal level   _____

4. To keep in my mind   _____

5. To make better   _____

6. To act in a certain way   _____

Name _____

At the Seashore

Find the meaning of each underlined word. Write the letter of the answer on the line.

Dear Pam,

I am at the seashore with my <u>parents</u> (____). The sea is so big and blue! It is <u>beautiful</u> (____)! I want to swim in the <u>surf</u> (____). But my mom says I have to stay in the <u>shallows</u> (____). I like to play in the sand, too. I have a pail and a <u>shovel</u> (____). I will make a sand <u>castle</u> (____).

Love,

Deb

a. where the water is not deep
b. mom and dad
c. a digging tool with a long handle

d. waves as they break on the shore
e. so pretty
f. a large house from the Middle Ages

Spell each word two times at the right.

1. parents

2. beautiful

3. surf

4. shallows

5. shovel

6. castle

Complete each idea with one new word.

1. It is safe to swim here

2. Where a queen lives

3. A mother and a father

4. Good to look at or listen to

5. I use this to dig with

6. I cannot swim there

Name _____

Pass It On

Find the meaning of each underlined word. Write the letter of the answer on the line.

I wrote a note. The note is for my friend. This is what the note says:

Dear Ted,

    Come to my house after you do your school <u>lessons</u> (____). We will have cookies and <u>juice</u> (____). I want to show you my new train <u>engine</u> (____). It is so cool! I want to be a train <u>engineer</u> some day (____). So I play with my engine a lot. That is my <u>hobby</u> (____). I want to <u>share</u> my hobby with you (____).

From,

Mike

a. homework
b. to use together
c. a fun thing to do

d. a drink from fruit or vegetables
e. a person who drives a train
f. the front part of a train that pulls the cars

Spell each word two times at the right.

1. lessons   _____   _____

2. juice   _____   _____

3. engine   _____   _____

4. engineer   _____   _____

5. hobby   _____   _____

6. share   _____   _____

Complete each idea with one new word.

1. An enjoyable activity for your spare time _____

2. Information that you need to learn or study _____

3. To divide something between two or more people _____

4. Something made from oranges or grapes _____

5. Someone who is trained to design, build or use machines _____

6. The machine that creates power to move _____

66

Name _____

In the Gym

Find the meaning of each underlined word. Write the letter of the answer on the line.

My friend likes to have P.E. in the gym. I do not like it very much. I like to have
P.E. <u>outdoors</u> (____). I think the gym is too hot and <u>stuffy</u> (____). I think the gym
floor is too <u>firm</u> (____). I think the sound in the gym <u>pounds</u> on the walls (____).
I feel like my head <u>hurts</u> from those sounds. (____). When we have P.E. in the gym,
I cannot <u>perform</u> very well (____).

a. to hit noisily
b. to have pain
c. outside in the open air

d. very hard
e. to do a job
f. without fresh air

···

Spell each word two times at the right.

1. outdoors   _____   _____

2. stuffy   _____   _____

3. firm   _____   _____

4. pound   _____   _____

5. hurt   _____   _____

6. perform   _____   _____

···

Complete each idea with one new word.

1. Strong and solid   _____

2. To be in a show   _____

3. Not inside   _____

4. Like a hammer sound   _____

5. To be in pain   _____

6. Closed up, without clean air _____

Happy Seeds

Find the meaning of each underlined word. Write the letter of the answer on the line.

Do you think seeds are happy? I do! I think seeds are very happy. The jobs of the seeds are to <u>produce</u> something pretty for us (____). That is why I call them happy seeds. They produce pretty things that make us happy, too. Some seeds produce flowers with a nice <u>aroma</u> (____). Some seeds produce green <u>lettuce</u> for us to eat (____). Some seeds produce grass for us to have a <u>picnic</u> on (____). Other seeds produce trees that grow apples or <u>plums</u> (____). Seeds are happy because they have an <u>important</u> job to do (____).

a. a big deal
b. to make something
c. a purple fruit

d. an outdoor lunch
e. a good smell
f. a salad vegetable

Spell each word two times at the right.

1. produce _____ _____

2. aroma _____ _____

3. lettuce _____ _____

4. picnic _____ _____

5. plum _____ _____

6. important _____ _____

Complete each idea with one new word.

1. A pleasant scent _____

2. To create _____

3. A rabbit likes it. _____

4. When dried, this fruit is called a *prune*. _____

5. A fun way to have lunch _____

6. It means something serious or powerful. _____

Top That!

Find the meaning of each underlined word. Write the letter of the answer on the line.

Some things look good on top. Did you every try these:

Put a gift in a box. Put a pretty <u>bow</u> on top (____).

Wear a winter coat. Put a <u>scarf</u> on top (____).

Put a block on a block. Put a <u>roof</u> on top (____).

Climb a mountain. Put a <u>flag</u> on top (____).

It is fun to put something on top. It gives a new look. It is a <u>chance</u> for art (____).

It is a chance to use your <u>talent</u> (____).

a. an opportunity
b. piece of cloth on a pole
c. the covering on the top of a house

d. a strip of material worn for warmth
e. a loop of ribbon
f. an ability or skill

Spell each word two times at the right.

1. flag

2. bow

3. scarf

4. roof

5. chance

6. talent

Complete each idea with one new word.

1. Playing good music, for example.

2. It keeps my neck warm.

3. It can have a pattern or other symbol on it.

4. A knot with loops

5. A favorable time

6. A bird can sit up here

Name _____

It Is a Seal's Life

Find the meaning of each underlined word. Write the letter of the answer on the line.

How fun to be a seal! To swim—to dive—to splash (____)! A seal has a nice life in the sea. A seal has all day just to swim and plunge down into the water (____). He can have any fish in the sea for his dinner (____). He can race and chase any seal just for fun (____). He gets wet, but wet is comfortable for him (____). A seal is glad to be a seal (____).

a. a good feeling
b. to dive into the water
c. to throw a liquid

d. the main meal of the day
e. to hurry after
f. happy

....

Spell each word two times at the right.

1. splash   _____   _____

2. plunge   _____   _____

3. dinner   _____   _____

4. chase   _____   _____

5. comfortable   _____   _____

6. glad   _____   _____

....

Complete each idea with one new word.

1. Not breakfast or lunch   _____

2. To go under water   _____

3. Not sad   _____

4. This makes me wet   _____

5. This can be a game   _____

6. A nice way to feel   _____

70

From Camp to Home

Find the meaning of each underlined word. Write the letter of the answer on the line.

Dear Dad,

I am at camp. I like camp, but I am <u>lonesome</u> for home (____). At

camp we get up early. We eat, and then we get very busy. We go to the

grass to <u>exercise</u> (____). Then we sit at a table to do our <u>craft</u> (____).

For lunch we eat a hot dog or <u>hamburger</u> (____). Then we read and take

a little <u>break</u> (____). Please pick me up <u>early</u> when you come (____).

Love,

Ben

a. a kind of artwork
b. to work the body
c. feeling alone

d. round, flat piece of cooked beef
e. not late
f. a rest from work

Spell each word two times at the right.

1. lonesome   _____   _____

2. exercise   _____   _____

3. craft   _____   _____

4. hamburger   _____   _____

5. break   _____   _____

6. early   _____   _____

Complete each idea with one new word.

1. Before the usual time   _____

2. Time to stop the work   _____

3. A work made using the hands   _____

4. A lonely feeling   _____

5. This is often served on a round bun, with ketchup _____

6. This can be stretching, running or other activity _____

Long Neck

Find the meaning of each underlined word. Write the letter of the answer on the line.

There is an animal with a long neck. It is <u>such</u> a very long neck (____). This animal has long, long legs, too. So this animal has a big <u>height</u> (____). The best lunch for this animal is to <u>munch</u> on a green leaf or two (____). In fact, it eats many <u>leaves</u> (____). It is not easy for this animal to get water. Its head is too far <u>above</u> the water (____). So, it gets water from the leaves. Do you know this <u>mystery</u> animal (____)?

a. to chew food
b. hard to understand
c. how high

d. over and up
e. more than one leaf
f. so much

....

Spell each word two times at the right.

1. such   _____   _____

2. height   _____   _____

3. munch   _____   _____

4. leaves   _____   _____

5. above   _____   _____

6. mystery   _____   _____

....

Complete each idea with one new word.

1. Something puzzling _____

2. Not below _____

3. Flat, usually green, parts of a plant or tree _____

4. Of that kind _____

5. Nibble noisily _____

6. How far up to the top _____

Big Stick

Find the meaning of each underlined word. Write the letter of the answer on the line.

My friend likes to walk. He likes to walk up and down the big hill in town. He always says, "I am going on a hike (____)." He takes a big stick with him. He says, "If I see a snake, that stick is my defense (____). That stick also keeps me steady so I won't fall (____)." My friend can hike a good distance (____). His big stick is his support (____). With his big stick he feels brave (____).

a. a way to hold
b. firm, stable
c. a long walk

d. strong with courage
e. how far
f. safety from attack

Spell each word two times at the right.

1. hike   _____   _____

2. defense   _____   _____

3. steady   _____   _____

4. distance   _____   _____

5. support   _____   _____

6. brave   _____   _____

Complete each idea with one new word.

1. Travel by walking   _____

2. Space between two things   _____

3. Not cowardly   _____

4. Something to help you keep from falling _____

5. Not shaky   _____

6. Something to protect me   _____

Hot Summer Day

Find the meaning of each underlined word. Write the letter of the answer on the line.

Most kids like a hot summer day. They like to feel hot, but they also look for a way
to <u>cool</u> off (____). There are many ways to cool off on a hot summer day. Some
kids jump off the <u>board</u> into the pool (____). That is a good way to cool off! Some
kids fill a <u>bucket</u> with cool water (____). Some kids run <u>under</u> cool water from a
hose (____). How do you cool off? Do you stand outside in a rain <u>shower</u> (____)?
Do you wait for a water balloon to <u>burst</u> (____)? What do you do?

a. not over
b. a large pail
c. a flat piece of wood or plastic

d. to become less hot
e. a short rainfall
f. to break open

....

Spell each word two times at the right.

1. cool   _____   _____

2. board   _____   _____

3. bucket   _____   _____

4. under   _____   _____

5. shower   _____   _____

6. burst   _____   _____

....

Complete each idea with one new word.

1. Dive off this into the pool.   _____

2. This feels very wet   _____

3. A container   _____

4. To break or explode   _____

5. Beneath   _____

6. Not warm or hot   _____

Name _____

In the Zoo

Find the meaning of each underlined word. Write the letter of the answer on the line.

Did you ever think about this? How did animals get into the zoo? The animals did not just run into the zoo. They did not walk or fly into the zoo. Someone <u>caught</u> each animal (____). Each animal was then <u>brought</u> to the zoo (____). It was never the animal's <u>choice</u> to go to the zoo (____). But the zoo is a good place to keep each animal safe. Each animal gets good care in the zoo. There is a good <u>diet</u> of food (____). There is <u>medicine</u> for the sick animals (____). There is a nice, dry place to sleep. The animals are happy, and they do not <u>complain</u> (____).

a. what you eat
b. the past tense of *catch*
c. the chance to choose

d. used to treat illness
e. to say you are unhappy
f. the past tense of *bring*

Spell each word two times at the right.

1. caught   _____   _____

2. brought   _____   _____

3. choice   _____   _____

4. diet   _____   _____

5. medicine   _____   _____

6. complain   _____   _____

Complete each idea with one new word.

1. The doctor may give this to you   _____

2. To find fault or whine   _____

3. A thing that has been selected   _____

4. A selected eating plan   _____

5. Grabbed   _____

6. I took something to a place   _____

To Run or Not to Run

Find the meaning of each underlined word. Write the letter of the answer on the line.

My brother loves to run. He is 10 years old, and he runs fast. Not <u>everybody</u> likes to run (____). Some people like to walk. Others like to skip. There are many <u>physical</u> things you can do (____). Physical <u>action</u> is good for your body (____). Physical actions bring more <u>oxygen</u> to your brain (____). Then you brain has more <u>ability</u> to think and to work (____). Physical work can help your <u>mental</u> work (____).

a. able to do
b. a colorless gas
c. something you do to get a result

d. of the mind
e. all people
f. of the body

Spell each word two times at the right.

1. everybody   _____   _____

2. physical   _____   _____

3. actions   _____   _____

4. oxygen   _____   _____

5. ability   _____   _____

6. mental   _____   _____

Complete each idea with one new word.

1. Each and every person   _____

2. To do with or done by the mind _____

3. Humans need this to breathe   _____

4. To do with the body   _____

5. Movement   _____

6. The power to do something   _____

76

Fun with Money

Find the meaning of each underlined word. Write the letter of the answer on the line.

Aunt Jill gave me a little can for my birthday. In the can there was $12 <u>cash</u> (____).
There was also a note that said:

Have fun with your cash! It is for you to <u>spend</u> (____). Just go spend it,
and <u>enjoy</u> doing that (____)! It is <u>possible</u> that I can give you more cash
next year (____). If I have a good job, I will <u>increase</u> your cash (____).

Do you like this gift from me? I <u>guess</u> that you do (____).

From,

Aunt Jill

a. to make more
b. to think so
c. to have fun

d. money
e. it might happen
f. to use money to buy things

Spell each word two times at the right.

1. cash   _____   _____

2. spend   _____   _____

3. enjoy   _____   _____

4. possible   _____   _____

5. increase   _____   _____

6. guess   _____   _____

Complete each idea with one new word.

1. To like what you do   _____

2. To grow in size or number   _____

3. Bills and coins   _____

4. To suppose   _____

5. Maybe or maybe not   _____

6. To pay for something   _____

Good for Your Nose

Find the meaning of each underlined word. Write the letter of the answer on the line.

Do you think that the nose likes good smells? There are many nice smells for the nose. A nice one is the <u>perfume</u> from a flower (____). Another good smell is from cookies still in the <u>oven</u> (____). New grass in the springtime is another <u>excellent</u> smell (____). To smell something is one <u>sense</u> that we have (____). The nose has <u>control</u> of the sense of smell (____). We cannot smell something with our eyes or ears. We <u>only</u> can smell with the nose (____).

a. power
b. just
c. stove

d. a good smell
e. a way to know something
f. very, very good

Spell each word two times at the right.

1. perfume   _____   _____

2. oven   _____   _____

3. excellent   _____   _____

4. sense   _____   _____

5. control   _____   _____

6. only   _____   _____

Complete each idea with one new word.

1. Better than very good   _____

2. *Sight* is one   _____

3. A pleasing odor   _____

4. An appliance used for baking _____

5. Be in charge   _____

6. Not more than this   _____

Name _____

In the Sky

Find the meaning of each underlined word. Write the letter of the answer on the line.

It is nice to look up in the sky. Sometimes the sky is all blue. Sometimes there are many white or gray <u>clouds</u> in the sky (____). The clouds move fast or slowly, and they <u>change</u> (____). Sometimes they move in a thin line. Sometimes they pile up and look <u>puffy</u> (____). White, puffy clouds look pretty. Dark, black clouds look <u>dangerous</u> (____). When you see dark, black clouds you must <u>dash</u> to a safe place (____). Keep your eyes on the sky. The clouds in the sky tell you about the <u>weather</u> (____).

a. light and fluffy
b. day-to-day climate
c. not safe

d. They hold rain.
e. to go fast
f. become different

··

Spell each word two times at the right.

1. clouds   _____   _____

2. change   _____   _____

3. puffy   _____   _____

4. dangerous _____   _____

5. dash   _____   _____

6. weather   _____   _____

··

Complete each idea with one new word.

1. A white or gray mass of water droplets suspended in the air _____

2. The condition of the outside air _____

3. To move quickly _____

4. To alter _____

5. A soft, fat look _____

6. Likely to cause harm _____

What to Eat

Find the meaning of each underlined word. Write the letter of the answer on the line.

School Lunch

Today's school lunch is fun to eat! It is beef and noodles. The beef and noodles are in a big <u>bowl</u> (_____). For your <u>fruit</u>, there is an apple (_____). For your treat, there is a <u>wedge</u> of cake (_____). You can <u>choose</u> milk or ice water to drink (_____). This is a nice lunch, and the <u>price</u> is $2 (_____). We will <u>offer</u> this same lunch next week (_____).

a. a piece that is thick at one end and thin at the other
b. a deep dish
c. how much to pay

d. a food with seeds
e. make a choice
f. put out something you can take

....

Spell each word two times at the right.

1. bowl   _____   _____

2. fruit   _____   _____

3. wedge   _____   _____

4. choose   _____   _____

5. price   _____   _____

6. offer   _____   _____

....

Complete each idea with one new word.

1. The cost of something   _____

2. Take your pick   _____

3. This can be a an apple, strawberry, orange, kiwi, grape, etc.   _____

4. Put soup or cereal in this   _____

5. Shaped like a triangle   _____

6. To suggest   _____

Slow Going

Find the meaning of each underlined word. Write the letter of the answer on the line.

There is an animal that cannot move fast. This animal is a slow animal. When it moves, it is "slow going." This <u>reptile</u> lives on land or by the water (____). It is not tall. It is very low. You can pick up a little one. A big one you cannot <u>lift</u> (____). This animal has something on its back. Because it has something on its back, it is slow, not <u>quick</u> (____). It can swim well. You can <u>often</u> find it by a lake (____). It swims in a <u>pond</u> (____). <u>Surprisingly</u> a big one can swim in the sea (____). Do you know what this animal is?

a. fast
b. amazingly
c. to pick up

d. a kind of animal
e. many times
f. little lake

....

Spell each word two times at the right.

1. reptile   _____   _____

2. lift   _____   _____

3. quick   _____   _____

4. often   _____   _____

5. pond   _____   _____

6. surprisingly _____   _____

....

Complete each idea with one new word.

1. A snake is one, too   _____

2. Ducks like to swim in this   _____

3. With great wonder   _____

4. To raise someone or something _____

5. Not slow   _____

6. More than one time   _____

Time at the Park

Find the meaning of each underlined word. Write the letter of the answer on the line.

For me, the best time to go to the park is after the snow falls in the winter (____).
We put out bread for the birds to eat (____). We also play in the snow. First, we
walk and walk in the snow to make a path (____). Then we run around the path.
The path has snow, so it is wet. Sometimes we slip (____). It is fun to slip in the
snow. We just laugh and get back up (____). We play and play until someone says,
"Quit (____)!"

a. a trail for walking
b. to fall down
c. a season of the year

d. to make a happy sound
e. stop
f. a baked food made from flour, water
    and yeast

....

Spell each word two times at the right.

1. winter   _____   _____

2. bread   _____   _____

3. path   _____   _____

4. slip   _____   _____

5. laugh   _____   _____

6. quit   _____   _____

....

Complete each idea with one new word.

1. This can be white, whole wheat, rye, cinnamon, etc. _____

2. Not summer   _____

3. This does not mean "start"   _____

4. Walkway   _____

5. Bigger than a giggle   _____

6. Take a spill   _____

Name _____

Home with the Card

Find the meaning of each underlined word. Write the letter of the answer on the line.

My teacher told us that today is a very big day. He said, "Today you will go home with the card!" We know that he means our report card. He said, "Be <u>certain</u> that you show your card to your mom or dad (____). Do not <u>hide</u> your card (____). You need to show the <u>truth</u> (____). If it is not a good card, do not be <u>afraid</u> (____). Your next card can be better. But you will have to make an <u>effort</u> (____). If you make an effort, I will be <u>aware</u> of that (____)."

a. to have fear
b. to keep from view
c. to know

d. to try hard
e. what is true
f. very sure

....

Spell each word two times at the right.

1. certain   _____   _____

2. hide   _____   _____

3. truth   _____   _____

4. afraid   _____   _____

5. effort   _____   _____

6. aware   _____   _____

....

Complete each idea with one new word.

1. Scared   _____

2. Not a lie   _____

3. To put out of the way   _____

4. Work   _____

5. To understand   _____

6. Without a doubt   _____

What Happened to the Plums?

Find the meaning of each underlined word. Write the letter of the answer on the line.

This story is about a kind of tree. It is a beautiful tree called a plum tree. Every year in the spring, this tree is all pink. It is pink because it is full of pink flowers. The pink flowers underline transform into plums (____). When the plums get big and sweet, someone comes to underline harvest them (____). This person puts the plums out in the sun to dry. As the plums dry in the sun, they get sweeter and sweeter. Soon, the sun will dry up the juice of the plums. Now they do not underline resemble plums (____). In fact, they are now called underline prunes (____). Prunes are good to eat, but some kids think they are underline awful (____). Try some prunes! They are good for your underline system (____).

a. a very dry plum
b. a group of things that work together
c. really bad

d. to make a great change
e. to look like
f. to gather crops

··

Spell each word two times at the right.

1. transform   _____   _____

2. harvest   _____   _____

3. resemble   _____   _____

4. prune   _____   _____

5. awful   _____   _____

6. system   _____   _____

··

Complete each idea with one new word.

1. A dried fruit   _____

2. To become something else   _____

3. Terrible   _____

4. To collect food that is ripe   _____

5. To be similar to   _____

6. An organized way   _____

Hot Spot

Find the meaning of each underlined word. Write the letter of the answer on the line.

My grandma lives in the desert, and I go to visit her there. She takes me for a walk around her house. It is a desert, and so it is very, very hot—especially in the summer (____). That hot sun makes my throat dry (____). So I take a water bottle with me. I want to drink a gallon of water (____). But a gallon of water is too much for me to carry (____). When we get back to Grandma's house, I run and turn on the faucet (____). Then I drink as much as I want. How could anyone survive in the desert without water (____)?

a. passage from mouth to stomach or lungs
b. swallow liquid
c. to bring

d. 16 cups
e. to live
f. mainly

....

Spell each word two times at the right.

1. especially _____ _____

2. throat _____ _____

3. gallon _____ _____

4. carry _____ _____

5. drink _____ _____

6. survive _____ _____

....

Complete each idea with one new word.

1. More than usually _____

2. To stay alive _____

3. Four quarts _____

4. Hold something and take it somewhere _____

5. Front of neck _____

6. To take in liquid _____

Name _____

Color Me In

Find the meaning of each underlined word. Write the letter of the answer on the line.

To color is what I like to do best. Sometimes I color in a coloring book. Sometimes I just get a white piece of paper. Then I make a <u>design</u> on the paper with my pencil (____). After that I begin to color my design. I like to use <u>lavender</u> (____). Then I <u>switch</u> to yellow (____). Next I fill in an <u>area</u> with pink (____). At last I use a <u>shade</u> of blue (____). I use other colors, too, until my design is <u>complete</u> (____).

a. the degree of darkness of a color
b. done
c. pattern

d. a pale purple
e. part of a place
f. to change

....

Spell each word two times at the right.

1. design   _____   _____

2. lavender   _____   _____

3. switch   _____   _____

4. area   _____   _____

5. shade   _____   _____

6. complete   _____   _____

....

Complete each idea with one new word.

1. The shape or style of something   _____

2. Finished   _____

3. A pale violet color   _____

4. Tint   _____

5. A certain space   _____

6. To trade   _____

Name _____

Old and New Ideas

Find the meaning of each underlined word. Write the letter of the answer on the line.

Do you know that *old* and *new* are <u>opposites</u> (____)? It is fun to think about opposite words. One word that is the opposite of *small* is <u>huge</u> (____). One word that is the opposite of *sad* is <u>merry</u> (____). How about *dry* and <u>moist</u> (____)? *Moist* is the opposite of *dry*. You can think about other opposites, like *slow* and <u>swift</u> (____). Think about words. Think about a lot of them. If you do not know a word for sure, use a <u>dictionary</u> (____).

a. a big book of words and their meanings
b. fast
c. a little wet

d. completely different
e. very big
f. happy

....

Spell each word two times at the right.

1. opposites   _____   _____

2. huge   _____   _____

3. merry   _____   _____

4. moist   _____   _____

5. swift   _____   _____

6. dictionary   _____   _____

....

Complete each idea with one new word.

1. Damp   _____

2. Use this to find definitions of words   _____

3. Not little   _____

4. Not alike at all   _____

5. Cheerful   _____

6. Speedy   _____

The Nice Things About Fall

Find the meaning of each underlined word. Write the letter of the answer on the line.

I like the summer very much, but there is a <u>season</u> that I like more than summer (____). It is fall. Fall is the time to pay <u>attention</u> to the trees (____). A tree's color can change from green in the summer to <u>rust</u> in the fall (____). Those colors make a pretty <u>display</u>. The trees are a beautiful display of color in the fall (____). I like to stand and watch a tree in the fall. Sometimes a leaf will come <u>floating</u> down (____). That leaf is a gift from <u>nature</u> to me (____). That is why I like the fall.

a. a reddish-brown color
b. to move in the air
c. a public show

d. one of four times of the year
e. careful thought
f. everything in the world not made by man

. . . .

Spell each word two times at the right.

1. season   _____   _____

2. attention   _____   _____

3. rust   _____   _____

4. display   _____   _____

5. floating   _____   _____

6. nature   _____   _____

. . . .

Complete each idea with one new word.

1. Moving lightly or easily   _____

2. All natural things   _____

3. Winter is one   _____

4. An exhibition   _____

5. A dark-orange color   _____

6. Concentration   _____

Jungle Jeans

Find the meaning of each underlined word. Write the letter of the answer on the line.

My <u>favorite</u> pants are my jeans (____). I call them my jungle jeans. That is because I like to <u>pretend</u> that I am in the jungle (____). In my pretend jungle, I go up in my apple tree. But I pretend it is a <u>banana</u> tree (____). I pretend to see a <u>monkey</u> in the tree (____). The monkey can <u>stretch</u> his arms to me (____). I am glad I have on my jungle jeans. With my jungle jeans on, I can <u>slide</u> down that banana tree (____).

a. long, curved, yellow fruit
b. an animal like a small ape
c. to cover a surface smoothly

d. most liked
e. make believe
f. to spread out to full length

Spell each word two times at the right.

1. favorite _____ _____

2. pretend _____ _____

3. banana _____ _____

4. monkey _____ _____

5. stretch _____ _____

6. slide _____ _____

Complete each idea with one new word.

1. A monkey eats it _____

2. The best-liked _____

3. Not real _____

4. To move easily _____

5. A chimpanzee is one _____

6. To make longer _____

Jungle Genes

Find the meaning of each underlined word. Write the letter of the answer on the line.

A jungle is full of animals. There are many <u>different</u> kinds of animals in a jungle (____). Each kind of animal is made of different <u>genes</u> (____). That is why some animals are big, and some animals are <u>tiny</u> (____). Some lizards have genes that make them small, but a gorilla has genes that make it <u>large</u> (____). Even bigger than a monkey is a <u>elephant</u> (____). An elephant is <u>gigantic</u> (____). It is gigantic because of its genes.

a. very small
b. very, very, very big
c. big

d. not the same
e. part of the cells found in all living things
f. large land animal

....

Spell each word two times at the right.

1. different   _____   _____

2. genes   _____   _____

3. tiny   _____   _____

4. large   _____   _____

5. elephant   _____   _____

6. gigantic   _____   _____

....

Complete each idea with one new word.

1. These determine how you look and grow. _____

2. Not big at all   _____

3. Not alike   _____

4. This animal has a trunk.   _____

5. Bigger than big   _____

6. Not small   _____

Actors in Action

Find the meaning of each underlined word. Write the letter of the answer on the line.

What is an actor? An actor is someone who puts on a play. An actor works on a place called a stage. What does an actor do? An actor does many things. First, he has to read his <u>script</u> (____). Then he has to learn when to smile and when to <u>frown</u> (____). He has to learn his <u>position</u> on stage (____). He learns when to speak to other actors. He learns what to <u>communicate</u> to them (____). <u>Finally</u>, the play is over (____). He learns to make his <u>exit</u> (____).

a. to look mad or unhappy
b. at the end
c. the way out

d. written text of a play, movie or show
e. to share information
f. the place where something is

....

Spell each word two times at the right.

1. script   _____ _____

2. frown   _____ _____

3. position   _____ _____

4. communicate   _____ _____

5. finally   _____ _____

6. exit   _____ _____

....

Complete each idea with one new word.

1. Not the way in   _____

2. At last   _____

3. Story for a performance _____

4. To bring the eyebrows together _____

5. Exchange information or feelings _____

6. Location   _____

Pick a Pumpkin

Find the meaning of each underlined word. Write the letter of the answer on the line.

The days are getting cool. The nights feel cold. Summer is over, and fall is here.
Soon the pumpkins will be <u>ripe</u> (____). I feel <u>eager</u> to pick a pumpkin (____). That
is something I just love to do. I will pick a pumpkin from the pumpkin <u>patch</u> (____).
I will take it to my house, and wash it in the sink. Then I will dry it and set it on the
table for everyone to <u>admire</u> (____). I will not <u>carve</u> a face on my pumpkin (____).
<u>Perhaps</u> I will put a little hat on it (____). A hat on my pumpkin would look so cute!

a. a small garden
b. ready to pick
c. to cut

d. ready to do something
e. to appreciate and enjoy
f. maybe

Spell each word two times at the right.

1. ripe   _____   _____

2. eager   _____   _____

3. patch   _____   _____

4. admire   _____   _____

5. carve   _____   _____

6. perhaps   _____   _____

Complete each idea with one new word.

1. To use a tool to cut   _____

2. Ready to eat   _____

3. Enthusiastic   _____

4. Possibly   _____

5. A small piece of land   _____

6. To like the way something looks   _____

Name _____

For My Trip

Find the meaning of each underlined word. Write the letter of the answer on the line.

I will need many things for my trip. Dad said to pack my <u>luggage</u> (____). First, I will pack my clothes. Then I will pack my socks and shoes. Then I will pack some books and puzzles to <u>entertain</u> me (____). I do not know what else to pack. Our trip will be to the lake, so maybe I will need <u>goggles</u> (____). I will pack a toy boat to play with on the <u>shore</u> (____). I will pack a fishing pole, but I will not pack <u>bait</u> (____). When I get to the lake, I will dig for bait and catch a <u>perch</u> in the lake (____).

a. to interest and delight
b. land along the edge of water
c. freshwater fish

d. small amount of food used to attract a fish
e. swim glasses
f. suitcases and bags

Spell each word two times at the right.

1. luggage   _____   _____

2. entertain   _____   _____

3. goggles   _____   _____

4. shore   _____   _____

5. bait   _____   _____

6. perch   _____   _____

Complete each idea with one new word.

1. You can eat this kind of fish   _____

2. Beach   _____

3. To amuse   _____

4. Special glasses to protect   _____

5. A fish will eat this.   _____

6. Pack this with things you will need on your travels   _____

Name _____

A Hairy Hare

Find the meaning of each underlined word. Write the letter of the answer on the line.

Do you know that a rabbit is also called a hare? A hare is a wonderful animal. It is covered with lots of hair. If you touch it, it feels <u>fuzzy</u> (____). It has a small tail that looks like <u>powder</u> (____). A hare jumps very well because its legs have <u>power</u> (____). The tall ears of a hare are able to <u>listen</u> to every sound (____). A hare likes to hop across a green <u>meadow</u> (____). A hare also likes to play in a big, wide <u>field</u> (____).

a. a field of grass
b. soft, white stuff
c. to hear and pay attention

d. strength
e. a piece of open land
f. furry

Spell each word two times at the right.

1. fuzzy   _____   _____

2. powder   _____   _____

3. power   _____   _____

4. listen   _____   _____

5. meadow   _____   _____

6. field   _____   _____

Complete each idea with one new word.

1. Hairy   _____

2. Open land used for growing crops or playing sports _____

3. Fluffy stuff   _____

4. Grassland   _____

5. To tune in   _____

6. Ability to do something   _____

Duck Water

Find the meaning of each underlined word. Write the letter of the answer on the line.

A lake is a good place for ducks. A pond is a good place for ducks. Even a pool is a
good place for ducks. That is because ducks need water. A duck feels at home in the
water. As soon as baby ducks <u>hatch</u>, they <u>enter</u> the water (____) (____). Baby
ducks know how to <u>paddle</u> in the water (____). Baby ducks <u>follow</u> their mother in
the water (____). A mother duck speaks to her babies with a loud <u>quack</u> (____). A
mother duck keeps her babies together in a <u>flock</u> (____)

a. to move through the water   d. come out of the egg
b. to go behind someone   e. duck group
c. duck talk   f. to go into

....

Spell each word two times at the right.

1. hatch   _____   _____

2. enter   _____   _____

3. paddle   _____   _____

4. follow   _____   _____

5. quack   _____   _____

6. flock   _____   _____

....

Complete each idea with one new word.

1. How a bird is born.   _____

2. A duck's sharp, loud sound   _____

3. Opposite of *exit*   _____

4. A group of animals of one kind that live, travel or feed together _____

5. To use the oars in a boat   _____

6. Not to lead   _____

Name _____

Lots of Cones

Find the meaning of each underlined word. Write the letter of the answer on the line.

Of course, everyone knows what an ice cream cone is. It is something cold and sweet to eat. But, do you know that there are many kinds of cones? A cone is a very <u>common</u> shape (____). A <u>funnel</u> is a kind of cone (____). I use a funnel to <u>transfer</u> birdseed from the bag into the feeder (____). Another kind of cone is a party hat. A party hat is a cone to wear when you are with other <u>guests</u> (____). A cone like a party hat makes everyone <u>grin</u> (____). You can even take a piece of paper and roll it into a cone shape. You will need <u>scissors</u> to cut off the point (____).

a. to move from one place to another
b. ordinary, regular
c. invited people

d. an open cone used to pour something into a narrow container
e. a cutting tool with two blades
f. to smile

....

Spell each word two times at the right.

1. common   _____   _____

2. funnel   _____   _____

3. transfer   _____   _____

4. guests   _____   _____

5. grin   _____   _____

6. scissors   _____   _____

....

Complete each idea with one new word.

1. Not so unusual   _____

2. Used to cut paper or fabric _____

3. A cheerful smile   _____

4. Relocate   _____

5. People who attend a party   _____

6. Because of the shape, a tornado is said to have this kind of cloud _____

96

At the Doctor's Office

Find the meaning of each underlined word. Write the letter of the answer on the line.

Next week I will have a doctor's <u>appointment</u> (_____). First, the doctor will check my <u>growth</u> (_____). She will see how tall I am and how big I am. Then she will listen to the beat of my heart. She will look into my eyes and ears. She will write everything on a <u>chart</u> (_____). She will ask me some <u>questions</u>, too (_____). I like my doctor very much. She is smart and nice. I want to know where she went to <u>medical</u> school (_____). Some day in the <u>future</u> I want to go to medical school (_____).

a. a sentence that asks something
b. how a person grows
c. a time set to meet

d. a way to show information
e. the time to come
f. to do with doctors or medicine

··

Spell each word two times at the right.

1. appointment   _____   _____

2. growth   _____   _____

3. chart   _____   _____

4. questions   _____   _____

5. medical   _____   _____

6. future   _____   _____

··

Complete each idea with one new word.

1. Increase of size   _____

2. A graph, outline, diagram or table   _____

3. These need answers.   _____

4. Not now and not in the past   _____

5. About medicine   _____

6. A scheduled day and time   _____

What's for Lunch?

Find the meaning of each underlined word. Write the letter of the answer on the line.

I take my lunch to school. I love to open my sack lunch at noon. I always find a <u>sandwich</u> there (____). That sandwich tastes so good to me! I find a <u>chunk</u> of cheese in my lunch sack, too (____). Cheese is a <u>wonderful</u> food (____). Cheese makes me <u>strong</u> (____). There is <u>another</u> food in my lunch sack (____). It is a cookie. When I eat my cookie, I save a <u>crumb</u> for a bird (____). A bird just loves my cookie crumb!

a. one more
b. powerful
c. a thick piece of something

d. causing wonder, amazing
e. tiny piece of bread or cake
f. two or more pieces of bread around a tasty filling

Spell each word two times at the right.

1. sandwich _____   _____

2. chunk _____   _____

3. wonderful _____   _____

4. strong _____   _____

5. another _____   _____

6. crumb _____   _____

Complete each idea with one new word.

1. A lunchtime favorite _____

2. Having great force _____

3. Really great _____

4. Rhymes with *hunk* _____

5. Some other _____

6. Tiny bit _____

A Night on the Boat

Find the meaning of each underlined word. Write the letter of the answer on the line.

My uncle has a boat. He took us for a boat ride. Then he said, "We will all sleep on the boat tonight." That was a fun night for me! I had my own <u>bunk</u> to sleep in (____). That bunk felt so <u>cozy</u> to me (____). I wanted to read a book in my bunk. So my uncle turned a lamp on. That lamp made a nice <u>glow</u> (____). Then my uncle said, "Lights out!" I was in my bunk with a <u>blanket</u> over me (____). I could feel the boat move back and <u>forth</u> (____). I <u>slept</u> very well that night (____).

a. a bed cover
b. a warm light
c. comfortable

d. to move ahead
e. narrow bed
f. fell asleep

....

Spell each word two times at the right.

1. bunk   _____   _____

2. cozy   _____   _____

3. glow   _____   _____

4. blanket   _____   _____

5. forth   _____   _____

6. slept   _____   _____

....

Complete each idea with one new word.

1. A steady, low light   _____

2. I sleep under this.   _____

3. Snoozed   _____

4. A small bed, often stacked   _____

5. Forward   _____

6. Snug and close and warm   _____

Cave Life

Find the meaning of each underlined word. Write the letter of the answer on the line.

What is it like to live in a cave? I think it is dark in there. I <u>wonder</u> if it is wet in the cave, too (____). I think that water <u>drips</u> inside a cave (____). Does the sun <u>shine</u> into a cave (____)? I do not think so. Then why did cavemen live in caves? It is because a cave is strong. A cave does not fall <u>apart</u> (____). A <u>storm</u> cannot break a cave (____). So cavemen had <u>shelter</u> there (____).

a. to fall like rain
b. to want to learn more about
c. into pieces

d. a safe place
e. strong weather
f. give off a bright light

....

Spell each word two times at the right.

1. wonder   _____   _____

2. drips   _____   _____

3. shine   _____   _____

4. apart   _____   _____

5. storm   _____   _____

6. shelter   _____   _____

....

Complete each idea with one new word.

1. To be curious about   _____

2. A protected place   _____

3. When liquid falls drop by drop   _____

4. Heavy rain, snow, sleet or hail with strong winds and,

   sometimes, thunder and lightning   _____

5. Not one piece   _____

6. Gleam or blaze with light _____

I Use a Map

Find the meaning of each underlined word. Write the letter of the answer on the line.

When my mom takes my sister and me for a ride in the car, I use a map. I like to see the way that we will go. I put my finger on the <u>highway</u> that we will use (____). Then I start to move it in the <u>direction</u> that we will go (____). Sometimes I ask my mom if we can go out of the city to the <u>country</u> (____). To drive in the country is what I like best. On my map there is a park in the country. That is where I want to <u>explore</u> (____). There is also a lake on my map. I want to find a way to that lake. My family can <u>wade</u> in that lake (____). When it is time to go home, I will use my map to help us <u>return</u> (____).

a. investigate, look all around
b. a main road
c. the way something is moving

d. away from town
e. to walk in the water
f. to go back

Spell each word two times at the right.

1. highway   _____   _____

2. direction   _____   _____

3. country   _____   _____

4. explore   _____   _____

5. wade   _____   _____

6. return   _____   _____

Complete each idea with one new word.

1. To come again   _____

2. To get the feet wet   _____

3. To travel in order to find out what a place is like _____

4. A major public roadway   _____

5. Opposite of *city*   _____

6. North, south, east or west   _____

Army Jeep

Find the meaning of each underlined word. Write the letter of the answer on the line.

My brother has a toy that I like. It is a little Army jeep. My brother lets me take that jeep outside. I push it <u>through</u> the grass (____). I push it up a hill and down into a <u>ditch</u> (____). I push it into the <u>thick</u>, wet mud (____). It does not get <u>stuck</u> (____). That toy jeep has four very good <u>wheels</u> (____). All that it needs is a good push from me. My brother is so nice to let me <u>borrow</u> it (____).

a. long, narrow trench
b. not thin
c. to use something that belongs to someone else, with permission

d. cannot move
e. round frames that turn on axles
f. in and out

....

Spell each word two times at the right.

1. through   _____   _____

2. ditch   _____   _____

3. thick   _____   _____

4. stuck   _____   _____

5. wheels   _____   _____

6. borrow   _____   _____

....

Complete each idea with one new word.

1. These turn around.   _____

2. Like a canal   _____

3. To take on loan   _____

4. Stay in the same place   _____

5. In one side and out the other   _____

6. Chunky, not slim   _____

In the Pack

Find the meaning of each underlined word. Write the letter of the answer on the line.

To go to school, a boy or girl must have a pack for the back. That is what we call a backpack. So many, many things go into the pack. It is not <u>light</u> (____). It is hard to carry. It has <u>everything</u> for the school day (____). It has an old pencil, and it has a new pencil that I have to <u>sharpen</u> (____). It has some <u>nickels</u> to pay for milk (____). The pack also has a lunch to eat. The lunch <u>might</u> have a cookie (____). One more thing is <u>necessary</u> for the pack (____). That is the homework!

a. money (five cents)
b. weighing a small amount
c. to make sharp

d. all of it
e. could
f. must have

Spell each word two times at the right.

1. light

2. everything

3. sharpen

4. nickels

5. might

6. necessary

Complete each idea with one new word.

1. Possibly

2. Not heavy

3. Have to

4. 5¢

5. To make a point on a pencil

6. Not just part

Name _____

Get Up and Go!

Find the meaning of each underlined word. Write the letter of the answer on the line.

It is a school day, and boys and girls cannot go slowly. Boys and girls really have to hurry (____)! There are so many things to do to get ready for school. First, you have to rise from your bed (____). Then, you have to decide what to put on (____). Afterwards, you need something to eat (____). After eating, you need to scrub your teeth (____). Now is the biggest challenge (____). Can you get to school on time?

a. to make up your mind
b. to get up
c. to do things fast

d. hard thing to do
e. clean by rubbing hard
f. later

....

Spell each word two times at the right.

1. hurry   _____   _____

2. rise   _____   _____

3. decide   _____   _____

4. afterwards   _____   _____

5. scrub   _____   _____

6. challenge   _____   _____

....

Complete each idea with one new word.

1. To move speedily   _____

2. Like a test   _____

3. To get out of bed   _____

4. To really make clean   _____

5. To come to a decision   _____

6. Not before   _____

TLC10410 Copyright © Teaching & Learning Company, Carthage, IL 62321-0010

Under the Leaf

Find the meaning of each underlined word. Write the letter of the answer on the line.

My friend Paul loves bugs. He tells me where to look for bugs. He says a good place to look for bugs is under a leaf. He always looks under leaves—<u>except</u> when there is snow (____)! He finds all kinds of bugs under leaves. The one he finds most often is the <u>caterpillar</u> (____). That is because the caterpillar <u>consumes</u> leaves (____). Paul also finds ants. Sometimes he finds spiders, too. Paul finds a <u>multitude</u> of bugs (____). He likes bugs. He never wants to <u>harm</u> them (____). He only wants to <u>observe</u> them (____).

a. eats or drinks
b. to look at closely
c. a large number of things

d. but not
e. a larva that changes into a butterfly or moth
f. to hurt

· ·

Spell each word two times at the right.

1. except _____ _____

2. caterpillar _____ _____

3. consume _____ _____

4. multitude _____ _____

5. harm _____ _____

6. observe _____ _____

· ·

Complete each idea with one new word.

1. This looks like a worm _____

2. Not just a few _____

3. Not in this case _____

4. To watch carefully _____

5. To eat a meal _____

6. Injure _____

A New Teacher

Find the meaning of each underlined word. Write the letter of the answer on the line.

When school begins again, most boys and girls will have a new teacher. Very often, children think a lot about that. This is what children <u>usually</u> ask, "Will my teacher be <u>strict</u>?" (____) (____) Children are <u>concerned</u> about that (____). It is not easy to start with a new teacher. Each teacher has a different <u>style</u> (____). Children learn from the teacher's style. But it takes time. It takes time for the children to <u>adjust</u> (____). So, when school begins, there is change. There is also a new way to <u>develop</u> (____).

a. worried
b. to grow
c. to get used to

d. most often
e. the way to do something
f. no-nonsense

•••

Spell each word two times at the right.

1. usually   _____   _____

2. strict   _____   _____

3. concerned   _____   _____

4. style   _____   _____

5. adjust   _____   _____

6. develop   _____   _____

•••

Complete each idea with one new word.

1. To adapt to a new way   _____

2. Advance, improve   _____

3. Frequently   _____

4. Habit or manner   _____

5. When the rules must be followed   _____

6. A troubled feeling   _____

In the Middle

Find the meaning of each underlined word. Write the letter of the answer on the line.

Summer is half over already. It is going so fast. It seems like it just started, but it is half over. Everybody is trying to get as much <u>pleasure</u> as they can (____). Some families are on <u>vacation</u> out of town (____). Other families are hard at work, but on the weekends they play. There is more time for fun, <u>no doubt</u> (____)! The water is so nice this summer. People can enjoy a <u>dip</u> in the pool (____). Other people enjoy a <u>sail</u> on the lake (____). Summer is half over. The <u>second</u> half of summer has begun (____)!

a. for sure
b. a short swim
c. after the first

d. a boat ride
e. good, happy fun
f. time off

....

Spell each word two times at the right.

1. pleasure

2. vacation

3. no doubt

4. dip

5. sail

6. second

....

Complete each idea with one new word.

1. A quick swim

2. Before the third

3. Time of rest and relaxation

4. A feeling of enjoyment

5. Without question

6. Sounds like *sale*

The Last Day of School

Find the meaning of each underlined word. Write the letter of the answer on the line.

It is the last day of school! <u>Hooray</u> (____)! Now, I feel some <u>relief</u> (____). I'm going to have a very <u>pleasant</u> summer (____). I will read a lot. I will write a lot. I will rest. I will draw. I will play and exercise, too. The difference is that I will do everything on my own <u>schedule</u> (____). I want to learn a lot this summer. I never want to stop learning, but I need a rest from school. I need a chance to <u>recover</u> (____). This year was a big <u>struggle</u> for me (____).

a. enjoyable
b. time plan
c. a happy shout

d. a hard time
e. to get better
f. freedom from pain or worry

··

Spell each word two times at the right.

1. hooray _____ _____

2. relief _____ _____

3. pleasant _____ _____

4. schedule _____ _____

5. recover _____ _____

6. struggle _____ _____

··

Complete each idea with one new word.

1. Timetable _____

2. A word used when people cheer _____

3. Very, very hard work _____

4. Comfort _____

5. Likeable _____

6. Improve in health _____

Name _____

Spelling Pre-Test Form

1. _____
2. _____
3. _____

4. _____
5. _____
6. _____

After you read the story and finish the lesson, draw a picture about the story here.

Name _____

Spelling Post-Test Form

1. _____   4. _____

2. _____   5. _____

3. _____   6. _____

....

Listen carefully as your teacher reads the story. Copy the story here.

_____

_____

_____

_____

_____

_____

_____

_____

_____

_____

_____

_____

_____

_____

Read pages
_____ to _____.
Write five
new words here.

_____
_____
_____
_____
_____

Keep track of
words you
don't know.
Look them up!

_____
_____
_____
_____
_____

Look for these
words in your
reading.

_____
_____
_____
_____
_____

I love to read!
I have read
these books.

_____
_____
_____
_____
_____

Award Certificates

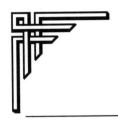

_____

has completed the vocabulary

assignments and is an official

Word Master!

Word Wise Award

Presented to _____

by _____

_____ certifies that

_____

has some awesome

Word Power!

Word Star Certificate

Presented to _____

by _____

for outstanding work!